DECODE YOUR DOG
second edition
By Den Cooke

Copyright and Reproduction Rights

Published: 2020 (second edition)
2018 (first edition)

Copyright © 2020 Pawsitive Press
ISBN: 978-1-8383012-0-0

pawsitive press
publications

11 Simpson Court
11 South Avenue
Clydebank
West Dunbartonshire
G81 2NR
pawsitivepress.co.uk

Chapter Index

Acknowledgements

Just over, two years on from the first edition of 'Decode Your Dog' this second edition has been comprehensively updated to add even more information on techniques to help better understand your dog and become even more confident and effective in training, or changing unwanted behaviours, in your dog.

With nearly 50 more pages than the first edition I have been able to include such things as adding three more ways to achieve loose leash walking bringing the total number of 'loose-leash walking' techniques to TEN! On top of this, amongst other additions, I have even included some information on dog 'Post Traumatic Stress Disorder' (PTSD) which, I have found, has become more pronounced in many dogs over the years and definitely the subject of much debate and misunderstanding.

No matter if you are a first-time dog guardian or you have had dogs all of your life, I am confident that you will find this book both interesting and enlightening. Even if you are a fellow dog professional, I am sure you will get real value from this book.

This book has been written, in an easy to digest format, that covers everything from what dogs do, and why, right through to how you can use this information to enhance your dog training and increase the bond with your furry friend.

This book, even the first edition of this book, would not have been possible if it were not for the help, guidance and patience of Michelle, my wife, who has been the bedrock of support and my inspiration for not only writing this book but that of becoming a full-time dog professional also.

I would also like to thank all of my clients, fellow professionals and, of course, the many dogs I have worked with over the years from whom I have always listened, learned and refined my techniques thus allowing my theories to become refined effective practices. I very much enjoy working with and learning lots from you all and, for me, the learning never stops. It was a big step moving from a part-time vocation to a full-time occupation but one that has been totally validated by the feedback, encouragement and support I have been lucky enough to receive.

Finally, I would like to thank both Darcy and Piper, my two Cocker Spaniels, who not only came into my world some years ago now but transformed it completely. Without them, and Michelle of course, I would not have made the leap of moving from a part-time interest and onto a full-time profession in the first place. Since taking the leap, I have never looked back and will continue to look forward with sustained excitement and optimism.

Thank you all.

Den.

Introduction

It may seem a bit strange to admit from the off, but my original specialist area is people not dogs. As an expert in reading human body language who also happens to own two Cocker Spaniels, I wanted to see if I could extend my skill set and learn to 'read' them in much the same way as I do people. I am a qualified NLP practitioner and someone who has studied people communication, body language, micro-expressions and even lie detection. I also have extensive people experience gained from my previous roles in sales and Senior Management.

Since leaving school, at 15 and with no qualifications, I have spent a lifetime absorbing myself in all things people and I have managed to achieve academic, career and personal success. From this, I felt that I could decode the world of dog in much the same way I have people and, by doing so, aim to build better support and development foundations and, of course, stronger dog-human-dog relationships. This desire took me into the world of dog behaviour and training theories, techniques and practices, both old and new.

On this journey, I found wide ranging incongruity of thought regarding causes for dog actions and the 'appropriate' remediation methods for dealing with undesired behaviour. Even the origin of dogs and how they originally formed relationships with humans remains hotly debated.

Recent studies have progressed apace with our understanding of dogs the shift of focus moving away from the 'Drill Sergeant' style of barking 'instructions' at a dog and trying to be the 'Alpha' of the pack. Modern research has advanced our understanding developing methods that work in tandem with the dog's agenda and motivating the desired responses rather than demanding them. This is a positive trend which, to me, coming from a people 'decoding' background makes perfect sense. Long may it continue.

Previously mentioned, in addition to a lifetime's experience of dogs, I have fully immersed myself in all things dog to become a fully qualified dog behaviourist. Over the past ten plus years I have accumulated over 12,000 hours of dog behaviour and training experience. In supplement I have absorbed a wealth of education through a myriad of books, workshops, training courses, videos, blogs and enjoyed experiential learning with a raft of dogs and people. I have also talked, in some depth, to many dog owners, trainers and behaviourists to canvass the widest possible range of thought, feedback and experiences. What a fascinating yet bewildering world I have found it to be.

The constant reward I get from this vocation is seeing how the changes and confidence growth (on the part of the dog and its guardians) positively affect the family dynamic. Quite often, unfortunately, I am called-in when families are at breaking point and they feel they have to turn to a dog professional as the last throw of the dice. It is, though, fantastic to witness, and be part of, the transformation journey, seeing dog/human relationships strengthened, stress levels lowering and fun times returning. I am so lucky and proud to play a small part in keeping so many families and their dogs together helping them to rekindle their newfound mutual enjoyment is immeasurably rewarding.

As with many people, my dogs, Darcy and Piper, are family members and I feel I must state that I do not see myself as their owner but moreover I am their guardian and teacher. Although I had paid money for my dogs, I don't own them. They are not my property but my kin. From the experiences I have had with my clients and others I have found that this viewpoint is common.

I mention the above because I want to make a clear distinction that some dogs are family dogs and others are raised as functional working dogs where their training and development requirements may be more formal and rigid. This book is aimed squarely at the domestic family dog. This is not to say I know nothing about working dogs because that is not the case, but over the years I have honed my expertise within the family dog arena and, for this book, I want to concentrate in this area. It is also not to say that working dogs are not loved as much as family dogs because nothing could be further from the truth. The only real difference is that working dogs have clearly defined jobs to do and they, in the main, need slightly different support mechanisms in place to enable them to perform such effectively and reliably.

The aim of this book is to give you, in a plain and jargon-free way, knowledge and understanding of how your dog views the world, how you can 'mind-tap' this view and implement proven techniques to gain an obedient and responsive dog, build positive behaviours and strengthen the bond between you and your dog. I am not looking to blind you with science, or pontificate on the origins of dogs, the science of dog learning theories or elaborate on the many different schools of thought but instead give you a solid 'working understanding' of the how dogs tend to view and interpret the strange world that surrounds them.

After reading this book you will be able to view matters from the dog's perspective and work within their reasoning methodologies in order to develop and shape desired behaviour outcomes.

Dog behavioural professionals have built their experience on understanding what dogs do and why. This is how they can get the results they do. My starting point, however, is trying to understand how dogs view, interpret and perceive all that surrounds them. I have tried to adopt this philosophy in everything I do.

I used to play poker at a decent level and I see a lot of similarities in the requirements of a good poker player to a good dog trainer or behaviourist. Any good poker play will have a solid knowledge of the game coupled with the ability to 'read' the thoughts and intentions of their opponent, mainly via their opponents previous actions and react accordingly. This basic understanding allows good poker players to get good results over time but it is only one aspect of the information decoding and, as such, can be pretty limited.

'Great' poker players take this a bit further and will add an understanding of how their poker opponents perceive them as a player. Taking this a step further a 'top level' poker player will not only have the ability to read their opponent but will do so whilst also understanding how their opponent reads them and add yet another level of what their opponent thinks the 'top level' player thinks of them. There is a whole lot going on often even before a card has been dealt.

To add further complications the players at the poker table will change regularly therefore so will the styles of play introduced continuously. This becomes perception versus perception within an active (changing) environment.

The information a poker player has to work with is imperfect yet top players repeatedly get positive results time after time. How is this possible and how does this relate to dogs? Well, poker players cannot ask their opponents what cards they hold therefore have to try and work this out for themselves. Top level poker players get results because they have an excellent core knowledge about the game. More importantly they will adapt their style of play to the constantly changing information around them and regularly review their perceptions if something is not quite working or some new information is presented. They do not get stuck in one style of play.

Their objective is to reward or disappoint their opponents in order to gain a constant advantage.

These players are always absorbing and adapting to the 'outcomes' and 'actions' on the table to maximise their control and influence. Poker professionals do not play cards they play situations. That's the secret to successful poker and also, believe it or not, dog development.

Dog experts as have to deal with 'imperfect' information in order to form a 'picture' of what is happening and why. Good dog experts will look, listen, learn and adapt in order to provide optimal programs for training or dog development. The key to success is applying training and techniques that are bespoke to the dog and not just generalist.

This is my preferred style of approach as I like to work to the dog's agenda and not mine. I do not come with one-size-fits-all solutions because I have found dogs to be as unique as people.

I will always try to manipulate the motivations and environment in order to guide the dog towards the desired outcome. I will always let the dog decide what option to take and reward the decision that meets with the best outcome for me and the dog. This approach allows the dog to almost teach itself and, given this, the dog will 'own' this behaviour which will stand a better chance of becoming embedded if regularly repeated and rewarded.

In fact, R J Hermstein noted that a behaviour that has been rewarded will have a 90% chance of being repeated (Hermstein's Matching Law (1961)). Edward Thorndike had also put forward a "Law of effect (circa 1898)" which stated that any behaviour that is followed by pleasant consequences is likely to be repeated, and any behaviour followed by unpleasant consequences is likely to be stopped.

'Choice' training, which is the basis of 'operant' conditioning, operates on the principle of associative learning where associations between events (or triggers) and outcomes are made by, in respect of this book, dogs and, how these reactions manifest themselves. These principles are especially true for dogs as they operate on very primal levels and don't complicate matters with self-perception, self-esteem or deceptions etc. Dogs act 'in the now' and always act 'honestly' within their own internalised view of the world. What you see is what you get, dogs pretty much wear their heart on their sleeve (if they had such a thing).

As an experienced dog behaviourist, in order to 'change' behaviour, I often create auto-motive responses that a dog has no (conscious) choice but to respond to. An auto-motive response is where the dog's brain directs an immediate behavioural response with no 'cognitive' processing by the dog. This is also called classical conditioning (Ivan Pavlov (circa 1904)). I will explain this and how to use it in more detail later in the book.

I promote and use approaches that I know will be receptive, and have meaning, to the dog. For dogs, I have found that the best learning is self-learning and, as previously noted, dogs can almost teach themselves, with guidance of course, via the 'guardian' rewarding correct decision making from their dog.

Although the above sounds great this book is not about me. I have written this book to share with you my knowledge, experience, philosophies and tips. My objective is to give you a greater understanding of the dog's motivations and how it perceives all that surrounds it, whilst giving you the tools to create your own successful training and behavioural modification programs. Furthermore, if you do feel you actually require a pet professional to help you then after reading this book you will be able to converse with them from a position of knowledge rather than ignorance. In the latter respect, it is not a point of failure should you need further professional help as, with the best will in the world, some dogs just don't respond to techniques that work for most other dogs and may require more bespoke guidance and support. To this end, I have put together a whole chapter on engaging a dog professional.

As a dog professional I have often been asked what is the difference between a dog trainer and a dog behaviourist? Not much to be honest. Certainly not much when it comes to the hours of learning, gaining experience, knowledge, professionalism and dedication from both. They are two sides of the same coin.

Quite simply, for me, a dog trainer introduces new behaviours to a dog whereas a dog behaviourist changes behaviours. Let me give you an example. A dog trainer will, let's say, 'teach' a dog to walk to heel. This is a new behaviour as the dog, in all likelihood, has never done this before. A dog behaviourist will be required when a dog has got a behaviour, which is undesired, and the guardian needs help to change or modify that behaviour. For example a dog that 'jumps up' on people.

I accept that this is an oversimplification but I am sure you understand the key difference between the two. I am also not saying that one is mutually exclusive to the other because that is not the case. However, changing behaviour often requires more bespoke planning taking account of the history and drivers for the given behaviour (which may not always be obvious) and changing the relationship between the behavioural stimulus and the dog.

Neither one role is better than the other and both are vitally important in supporting a dog's development but I do get asked frequently about the difference so I thought it wise to add my 'tuppence worth' here. It is a hotly contested area but, for me, it is simple.

Trainer or behaviourist, all I would want, if in need, is a qualified and skilled dog professional who is knowledgeable, caring and empathetic who looks at my dog as 'patient zero' and works up from there and adapts, when needed, to arising changes ensuring the best solution(s) possible are afforded MY dog. Yes, you will often pay more for a dog behaviourist over a dog trainer but the unpicking of the undesired behaviour and remodelling it into desired behaviour does take time and time, as we all know, costs money.

While I am here, I also want to give you my thoughts on the, increasingly popular, dog behaviour television programs that often show 'quick fixes' to issues that the dog expert achieves in 30 minutes or less. In short, they don't. It is a con and sets unrealistic expectations for their viewers. Again, let me explain.

The television program is wholly pre-planned. Everything from the type of shots through to the required outcome. The dog expert is supported by 'researchers' and other experts from the television company who will have been in close, and constant, communication with the family priming them, readying the environment and agreeing on what issue, or issues, are to be 'tackled'.

The dog expert will then address the issue ensuring that there is a semblance of a 'positive outcome' that can be filmed. The journey to that point, although filmed, will be heavily edited in order to fit in the required time slot. Neither the family nor the expert will steer from the agreed narrative. After the filming has completed all the crew, expert and director etc will leave. For the standard follow up (self-filmed) element a plan will have been given to the family in order to continue what was covered. No more no less.

The family will still need to do the work after the dog expert has left. There is no quick fix and what has been achieved still needs to be practised in order for the dog to adopt the new rules as part of its daily routine. If the family did not do this then everything achieved would have been lost probably within 24 hours of the expert leaving. Even the 'tv family' have to put in the work as there are no short cuts, irrespective of what miracles the tv dog expert proclaims. I know that this may seem a bit of a whinge, and I suppose it is, but honestly, in dog training and development you definitely reap what you sow. Please don't believe the hype.

Anyway, moving on, dogs have been around people for over 12-15,000 years and throughout this time our reliance on them and their reliance on us has become entrenched. Dogs have become domesticated to the point that they would not be able to survive and thrive if we were not there for them. In fact, even the dog's brain has 'evolutionarily' changed to the point that most dogs crave human interaction as a 'need'. Such interactions will release a flood of dopamine (the pleasure chemical) into the dog. The relationship between human and dog is almost symbiotic.

As humans, we have selectively bred the dogs for different tasks such as herding, hunting, guarding etc but even after all these years, our knowledge of what makes them tick is in the main, relatively fetal in respect of what we know of other animals. It is profound that fewer studies have been conducted in dogs, and dog psychology, than that have been conducted in the wider animal kingdom. This is beginning to change though.

Conversely, our dogs never stop learning about us and over the decades and centuries their knowledge of people has arguably become almost greater than our knowledge of people. They can read people and situations very accurately and relate events and actions to positive or negative outcomes.

I would advocate though, that even with the above being said, we do still need to give them space and time in order to for them to absorb the environment that surrounds them. To this end, the best starting point is allowing the dog to learn about us. That might sound a bit strange but it is really not.

If you think about it, dogs are dropped into alien environments full of strange creatures (us) and expected to adapt successfully from the off. There is little, or no, pre-conditioning for most dogs, apart from their genetics and they are whipped away from their mum and siblings right smack in the middle of their initial development period whilst their brain is still forming.

Dogs, as do people, tend to feel more comfortable in those that they 'trust'. Therefore, you should give them the opportunity and space to explore you. To do this, I would recommend that you sit somewhere comfortable, relax, say nothing and allow your dog just do its thing and explore you and everything around you. Even if you have had your dog for years this exercise is still beneficial as you may find that you will learn as much about your dog as your dog will about you. I know you will find this a strange exercise but it is amazing how often our talk and actions get in the way of observing, learning and understanding. It astounds me that this crucial aspect of human-to-dog-to-human absorbance is overlooked so often by so many.

In this book you will also find out how silence is such a vital and effective training tool! I call this 'dynamic silence' and it is a crucial component of training.

In respect of training techniques, I have found, in my experience that there is no one solution that works for all. Dogs are, breed aside, the same but different. You really do hold all the cards in shaping your dog's behaviour albeit good or bad. You will have the knowledge of the environment and lifestyle in which both you and your dog live within, therefore you will be able to deliver training that better reflects you and your dog's personality and context. Dogs are a pretty good mirror to the life and lifestyle they live within.

What I mean by this is that a behaviour may seem similar from one dog to another but often the context and motivation driving that behaviour is different. It is also important to remember that it is not the destination (behaviour) but the journey (motivation) that you need to understand and address if you are to have any real chance of creating positive change. As humans, far too often we focus on the behaviour and not the cause. This book will give you the tools to understand the journey AND the destination.

I also believe that dogs retain strong natural intuition in things, people and situations. In fact, dogs are almost telepathically intuitive and tend to know what is going to happen, often before we do. I strongly believe that we also had similar attributes when we were young but invariably lost these as we grew older as they were not evidently required (or valued).

Furthermore, to a dog, everything, from people to inanimate objects right on through to the actual space that surrounds them, has a value which could be called a 'survival resonance'. This is the primal foundation through which they view their world and one that, along with their experiences, genes and breed, helps shape their character and personality. In respect of 'genes' or breed traits I will go over this in more detail later in the book.

In this book, you will learn more on how dogs view the world and what motivates them but I will not blind you with science or jargon as I want to keep this book as unacademic as possible. I want to give you a good solid foundation to understanding the language of people filtered via the dog's perspective rather than create an academic, convoluted, jargon laden tome embedded with constant (further) study references. I will note some of the sources I have used in compiling this book in the references chapter at the end but do so in order to give you the opportunity to read more should you wish to do so but not as required reading. If this is the type of book you are looking for then great - this book will deliver!

As there will be a lot of information covered, I will put a bullet point summary at the end of each chapter of the key points of each chapter.

So let's begin.

Chapter 1: Engagement

Okay so you have a dog. Your dog is going to naturally bond, engage and adapt to you by default as it lives with you and you are both entwined in each other's lives? Well, yes and no.

Your dog is a sponge and it does look for ways to naturally assimilate into its environment but it is not that simple. Be it a puppy or an elder dog they will observe and adapt with, or without, direct guidance from you. You see, your dog will interpret everything it sees and hears into its own survival and reward plan (survival resonance). The central, and only, character in a dog's world is the dog itself. I accept that as dogs are domesticated and bred to be social this may seem a bit of a strange statement. Although dogs are predisposed to want to please their guardian, dogs primarily operate on a "what's in it for me" basis and act, or react, accordingly.

Dogs think and feel on a very primal level and 'link' positive and negative experiences developing its own life-plan (or coping strategies). A dog will display the behaviours it feels are right for the given situation, or situations, it finds itself in. Further to this, via learned experiences, a dog will develop a register of actions and consequences. It is important to remember this when trying to understand 'why' a dog does what it does.

As stated, the basic tenet for a dog is "what is in it for me". If you view a dog as a permanent and demanding 2-year-old toddler with ADHD and add to this great intelligence, almost spiritual level intuition, amazing senses and forensic level observation capabilities, then you start to understand what drives and motivates a dog and how equally capable they are of achieving great things or creating great disasters.

As it is with people the above reflects most, but not all, dogs and the range in these abilities can be quite wide. Generally though, dogs have refined their cognitive processing capabilities to ensure that they survive and thrive within our modern 'domestic' environments.

The primary question in a dog's world is "what's happening here?", "what is the likely outcome?", "what is in it for me?", "what did I do previously in the same situation?", "is this going to be good or bad experience (outcome perception)?" and "can I cut to the chase (get the reward quicker or get away/avoid the negative immediately)?".

This thought process happens almost instantaneously. I call this an 'activity-chain' and it is an almost intuitive process. An example of this would be that you may have just got up off the couch to get your coat intending to take your dog for a walk. Your dog will have already worked out that he/she is going for a walk, often before you have even put your shoes on or grabbed the lead! What we do at the start of an activity-chain your dog has already concluded and pictured the outcome. He/she has worked it out, correctly or incorrectly, and is now (probably) aroused in anticipation!

It is also of vital importance that we understand our dog is a dog and not a human nor a domesticated wolf. All too often we humanise (anthropomorphise) dog behaviour placing human emotions or rationales (guilt, shame etc...) on what we see. However, a dog is not capable of understanding the concept of right, wrong, shame, guilt etc therefore such anthropomorphisms don't make much sense and are often counter-productive. It is important to understand that everything your dog does is right – to the dog anyway. It is only when those behaviours clash with our own standards of what we view as acceptable then this becomes an issue.

This is where corrective actions are required. Corrective action sounds quite harsh but it need not be, and should not be, punitive and the best corrective actions are the ones where the dog is incentivised and motivated to give the desired behaviour in place of the previous negative behaviour. The aim for us humans is to embed the positive changes into the dog's character and its own internal survival framework.

This type of approach ensures consistent, reliable and long-term positive results. However, note I have not stated 'permanent' results as very little is permanent with a dog as it operates "in the now" and motivations need the occasional and random (positive) reward reminder in order to maintain and solidify the behaviours you want (habituation).

So what to do? Well, as indicated previously, in the first instance do absolutely nothing – no touch, no talk, no (direct) eye contact. Let the dog explore you (and the environment) and you just observe. Even if you have had your dog for years this is not a bad reset exercise. This will become our baseline. When I say 'just' observe I don't really mean 'just observe' as this is not a passive exercise. You should be looking for positive and negative indicators. This will enable you to establish your approach when looking to understand/modify behaviours.

Believe it or not, dogs can be introvert, extrovert, optimistic, pessimistic, confident, over-confident, attention addicted, person addicted (over reliance) etc and understanding these character traits will help you understand what motivates and drives your dog. Dogs can also change from optimistic to pessimistic and vice versa resulting from their experiences and previous outcomes. With this information you can change negative behaviours into positive ones.

Here is an inexhaustive and indicative list of things to look for: -

Positive (Possibly extrovert, optimistic, confident, over-confident)
- Play bows
- Head up and eyes bright
- Tail down and relaxed

- Ears up (but not forward)
- Mouth open slightly, relaxed & tongue exposed
- Tail wagging (warning: see note below)
- Bum wagging (the Tina Turner shuffle) <although if dog is trying to make itself small at the same time then this is (negative) appeasement behaviour
- Focus on you
- Relaxed coat (no hackles up, skin not tight)
- Loose stance (not fixed, rigid etc)
- Bouncing when running around
- Interacting with others

Negative (Possibly introvert, pessimistic, unconfident, fearful, over-attached)
- Looking away
- Lip licking
- Panting
- Yawning
- Ears up & forward (or down and back if ready to attack)
- Fixed gaze
- Wide eyes (whale eye (showing a lot of white in the eye as if looking around their back without moving their head)
- Hackles up
- Tightness of skin/coat
- Growling

- Snarling and barking
- Showing teeth
- Lips curled or possibly mouth closed tight
- Lunging forward
- Tail tucked in between legs (some dogs, such as greyhounds, do this as a norm therefore you cannot apply this aspect to them).
- Tail stiff and up or horizontal (tail may quiver)
- Tail wagging (see below)
- Head down (front of body may lower also)
- Avoiding, or creating space from, others
- Following, to the exclusion of others, one person/dog

As I say the above is only indicative as there are many more signs for both positive and negative but the point here is just to give a quick overview of signs and possible basic interpretations.

You can test if your dog is optimistic or pessimistic quite easily. Assuming your dog is treat orientated, and most dogs are, then using a Kong or puzzle toy, place a treat in the toy that you know will be extremely difficult to extract. If your dog gives up after about 10-30 seconds and looks over at you (for help) then you are likely to have a pessimistic dog. However, if your dog stays at it, almost to the point of obsession, then you have an optimistic dog that believes in its own abilities to get something done rather than look for help.

Testing for introversion or extroversion is even simpler. It is not just about whether a dog interacts with other dogs/people or not. If your dog enters new experiences without a care and relishes finding out more and exploring nooks and crannies then you have an extrovert dog. If your dog generally stays tight close to you and would rather edge into new experiences slowly, cautiously, or not at all then your dog is an introvert. Simples.

Measuring confidence is a bit more of an art rather than a science because your dog may be confident in one situation but not another. Basically, if your dog generally bounces around with a loose body/skin/coat, head up and tail wagging then that is a happy confident dog. Conversely if your dog more often than not has its head down, tail tucked between its legs, looks away constantly, lip licks, yawns, makes itself look small and keeps its distance from you then you may have a dog that is not-so-confident and possibly stressed.

You should be able to ascertain if your dog is happy and confident or nervous and not-confident just by the way it moves around you and the area you are in. To complicate matters a bit more the above is not set in stone and some behaviours, such as tail tucked in, assuming your dog has a tail, may be breed specific (as noted previously greyhounds natural tail tucking) and can be observed in both positive and negative emotions.

A good test to conduct for anxiety/stress is to offer a small treat that you know it likes. If the dog is reluctant to take the treat they may not yet be fully at ease. Survival, against a threat, real or perceived, is of greater importance than taking a treat.

The above also assumes a dog in good health and in an inert (neutral) environment. If in doubt, get your dog vet checked and be aware of the environmental influence on your dog. Also, beware that dogs are good at masking pain/stress etc, as this is viewed as weakness within the pack, so it may not always be obvious. It may seem a bit of an obvious statement but pain and discomfort will always affect behaviour and skew any observed responses.

Note: a wagging tail could often be false flag indicator as dogs could wag their tail when they are both happy and agitated. The key here, as with reading people, is to look at everything in context and absorb a cluster of information rather than focus on any particular aspect.

You will note that I have said nothing about dominance. Dominance and the 'alpha dog' theory I view as myths which, for some reason, has taken hold and is still considered fact by 'old school' dog professionals. I am not a subscriber to this train of thought. In fact, Professor Rudolf Schenkel, who first coined the phrase "alpha male" in his book 'Expressions Studies on Wolves (1947)' where he had 'observed' such behaviour via his study. This was a flawed study though as he had used a group of 'captive' and 'non-family pack' wolves whose behaviour was markedly different from the actual natural behaviour that would come from wolf packs 'in the wild'. Eventually, after the completion and publication of this study, Professor Schenkel realised that the 'alpha' theory was actually incorrect in respect of wolf packs and he has since spent most of his life since trying to debunk this precept. Unfortunately, it appears that, at time of writing, he has still not achieved this which is, for me, disappointing. For the record, ironically, although wolf packs may have pack leaders, which is usually the parents, wolves live in family groups and work together sharing roles, responsibilities and resources to guide the whole pack to work cohesively ensuring all are safe and well fed etc. Aggression rarely forms part of the control mechanism within a wolf pack.

I view what is often coined 'dominance' as confidence. For dogs there are no set, or changing, hierarchies in place, egalitarian or otherwise and to think so is plainly ridiculous. Many other animals in the wild, but certainly not all, do have alpha structures in place whereby the use of physical force (dominance) to establish control and access to scarce resources and mating opportunities (survival of the fittest) are the norm. However, dogs have been domesticated for so long that there is no need to fight for either food or the right to mate, in fact, dogs are predominantly mating matched by humans.

Dogs also live, in the main, independently of other dogs therefore the need to be the 'alpha' has long since diminished. The thought that a dog is trying to dominate a human is, quite frankly, laughable and, in my opinion, both counter-intuitive and counter-productive. If you take a Darwin view of gene adaptation over the generations then the need to be the alpha would have no doubt been bred out of the dog species a very long time ago as it no longer serves as a survival need. Even if that was not the case there are no survival conditions, nor living requirements, for any dog requiring it to become the 'alpha'. In fact, human interaction, for most dogs, is THE survival 'need' and it is craved much in the same way as food and water.

This understanding has been born out via a study in Russia, set up by Lyudmila Trut called the silver fox domestication experiment, which to date, has been going on for over 60 years and counting. In this study, which started in 1959, random wild foxes were captured and mated. In each litter generation only the 'people friendliest' foxes were allowed to mate with other 'matched' people friendly foxes. At the same time, as part of a different study group, the less people friendly foxes were also matched against foxes of similar temperament and mated.

The experiment has shown that the more generations of people-friendly foxes were produced the more 'dog like' the foxes became and the more they craved human interaction whilst the non-people-friendly bred foxes continued to remain aloof.

The experiment has shown that, much as with most dogs, not only does each (people-friendly) fox generation desire human interaction it has been proven that the foxes NEED human interaction else they become depressed. Human interaction with these foxes releases both dopamine and oxytocin chemicals in the fox giving it both pleasure and a desire to bond. This has shown that the craving for the bred 'people-friendly' foxes to be with humans satisfies both a biological and psychological 'survival' need.

Remember, us humans provide all of the resources for dogs therefore there is just no gain to be had being fully 'independent' therefore no need for alpha structures. Dogs are, of course, primal in thought and operate only to the principle of 'what's in it for me' (which I will go into more detail later in this book).

Dogs are opportunists and independent in desire therefore they will always try and work out the best way to get what they want, or get away from what they don't like, irrespective of any 'dominant' or 'confident' dogs that may be within 'their pack'. It may be semantics to use the term 'confidence' instead of 'dominance' but far too often for my liking dominance has been used as a defence for using fear and force to train dogs. For me, call it want you want, but the main point I would like to make is that I don't support force and fear approaches and I know, from experience, that you don't need to use such in order get results. All you need to be is aware of is primal desire principles, basic dog language and how our dogs understand us and the environment in order to keep your dog safe, happy, well trained and focused.

I see the pack, which for me is the dog(s) within the family group, as one team with shared goals of happiness, safety, security and sustenance. Much alike bringing up our kids, using education, guidance and boundaries we, as guardians, set out our expectations of what is acceptable and what is not. As you will see in the next chapter "How Dogs Learn" it is not at all a laissez faire approach to achieving positive results but more over a true partnership with shared goals.

Dogs, unfortunately, do not come pre-loaded with the instructions for modern life therefore we need to help them learn these via the deployment of motivation and incentivising techniques. Physical or psychological punishment is never acceptable. There is absolutely no need. It is not 'force first' but 'force free' that I believe gets real and lasting results. In fact, in my experience, old school training can actually bring on unwanted behavioural reactions via fear-based responses.

ENGAGEMENT CHAPTER SUMMARY

- **Bonding**
- **Survival resonance**
- **What is in it for me?**
- **Primal Thinking**
- **Dog reasoning and outcomes**
- **A dog is a dog**
- **Observation exercise**
- **Positive and negative behaviour**
- **Dog optimism and confidence**
- **The dominance myth**
- **Force free training**

Chapter 2: How Dogs Learn

In chapter one, I stated that dogs observe us and look to blend into their environment as seamlessly as possible. Notwithstanding, seamlessly to them and not always to us.

They are masters at the art of observation as well as being indisputable body language reading experts. Couple their sharp eyesight with superb hearing (what you can just hear at 15-20 feet and dog can easily hear at 60 feet), and along with the super-human ability to smell, even the faintest of odours, then they are a force to be reckoned with when it comes to environmental and situational analysis. Just with smell alone, given that they have circa 300 million receptor cells and independently operating nostrils they can segregate smells even when breathing out and can detect 'trace scents/odours' days after the scent has been laid. From this, dogs gather a lot of information, about other dogs and the environment almost instantaneously. Impressive to say the least.

So dogs have a good sense of smell – which is good but how does that translate to 'how dogs learn'? Well, funny you should ask. Dogs learn a lot about their surroundings via smell. We know that dogs like to get up close and personal with the rear ends of other dogs along with having a predisposition for a good old inspection of bums, pee and poo but you will be surprised what information they get from this. It is generally accepted that dogs can 'read' the sex, maturity (not age per se), temperament (energy level), health and stress levels of other dogs via the smell of other dog's pee and, for me, if they can get this information from pee then there is no reason why they cannot garner the same from poo.

This can be the case days, if not weeks, after the nasty business has been released upon the world. For those that know this already you may note that I have omitted status (or rank/dominance) which is considered by some to be another element that dogs can detect via smelling pee etc. However, not for me. I just don't buy it as for status or rank (hierarchy/alpha) to actually have any real meaning then a dog has not only got to have a sense of self, but also a sense of others within fixed hierarchical structures. No, as I say I don't buy it given what I understand of the primal logic that I believe dogs work to. The status argument just does not stack up. The principles of the same argument also apply when it comes to dogs interpreting breed from smell as I don't think it is plausible but I do have an open mind on this. Species, yes, breed not so much.

On the subject of pee and poo you may be surprised to learn that circa 30-40% of dogs have a propensity to eat poo (coprophagia). Given this it is sensible that you are not too harsh on your dog that eats its own poo – it's disgusting to us but viewed as perfectly acceptable to some dogs as they can smell the nutrients still residing in the poo. Dogs, from what I understand (although I am not a vet) have digestive systems that are quite poor at extracting all of the nutrients first time around from what they eat so, when they decide to have a poo nibble, it is almost like having double helpings! That being said, not only you do need to be careful when your dog eats other dog's (or other animal) poo, as it may contain bacteria that could upset your dog's digestive system, but your dog may then come over to lick your face straight after, Yuk! Disease and bacteria can especially be present if the dog or other animal that had originally evacuated was not in full health at the time.

If your dog does exhibit coprophagia then I would recommend initially checking that its current diet is providing the sustenance and nutritional requirement it needs and, if all good in this respect, arranging a full vet check just to rule out any health issues that may have led to the dog's desire to eat poo.

This all being said, prevention and redirection (incentivising alternatives) is key here in stopping, or reducing the tendency for your dog to want to partake in coprophagia activities. You will need precision timing in pre-empting or redirecting the behaviour and offer a better option for your dog to take. What you don't want to do is shout, swear or show the angry face as this is not likely to result in the outcome you are looking for but, instead, it could lead to the creation of a craftier and quicker (in the execution of eating the poo) dog.

As for rubbing a dog's face in pee to deter this from happening again well, again, this is poor logic. Again, pee and poo is obviously disgusting to us but to a dog it is not. Rubbing a dog's nose in its own pee is a wholly fruitless endeavour. Further to this, unless you actually catch your dog in the act, then your dog will not make the connection of the punishment to the crime as the (pee) moment has long gone and your dog's mind will have totally moved on from that event. The rubbing of the nose correction may create fear as it will be coupled with your disapproving tone and harsh actions which may eventually change the behaviour but with this type of fear approach it is almost guaranteed to create a more nervous, cautious and possibly craftier dog.

Finally on this subject, you will be glad to know, a little bit more about dogs scent marking (chemical communication). Although there is currently no definitive (science based) reasoning as to why domestic dogs still scent mark, for me it is not a sign of dominance but moreover a need to lay a familiar scent as a type of calling card and, very often, to give the dog some comfort and security within their 'marked' territory. The stronger their own scent smell is in an area, the more 'at home' they will feel.

Further, a dog scent marking an object such as a toy is likely to be because there is some sort of opposing scent on the item and they wish to neutralise this and place their own scent on it. It is not a mark of ownership per se as dogs, by default, wish to own (have) everything they see anyway and to have such all of the time. For ownership to have any real resonance would mean that other dogs would have to understand the concept of 'ownership' respect the scent 'flag' or 'own' it themselves by peeing over the previous mark before taking it. However, dogs just don't see it that way. A pee 'marked' toy has as much chance of being picked up by another dog as a non-marked toy.

Although it is primarily unneutered male dogs that scent mark it is not exclusively an unneutered male dog pursuit as neutered males may do this also. Even some female dogs scent mark. Dr Anneke Lisberg (Chemical Communication in Domestic Dogs (Lisberg & Snowden (2009)), has studied this area and identified differences in high tail dog scent marking to low tail dogs but it is probably fair to say that more questions than answers have arisen as a result. In my experience I have found that dogs who tend to 'mark' more than others also tend to be generally less secure/confident (cautious and possibly reactive) and like to place scent marks down to place their scent on an unknown object, or perceived territorial boundary, in order to provide some environmental security. Thereafter, if this activity is repeated continually, it becomes learned behaviour and habituated as part of a dog's coping mechanism. But I digress.

So what does all this mean? As stated already, let's think primal. Although dogs are great at predicting outcomes they can only really focus on one thing at a time. A dog cannot multi-task and always looks for an 'immediate' or 'imminent' outcome from the thing, or activity, that has got its attention at the time. It will zone out everything else unless, for some reason, a distinct 'distraction noise' cuts through its focus and it immediately but temporarily disengages

dogs the imprinting and socialisation period ends around 16 to 18 weeks.

If a dog is removed from its litter before 8 weeks it will miss out on vital social and cognitive development not just over the next crucial 8-10 weeks but probably for life. The dog's brain may not fully develop which will potentially, and probably, cause behavioural issues in later life.

However, assuming you get your new pup at 8 weeks, then it will naturally look to continue learning life's lessons from you. You are now mum. Good puppy engagement is vital to having a content, confident and acceptably curious dog. The key to successfully achieving this is to allow your puppy to experience everything, from people, dogs and new places, and show plenty of praise for the things you like and (positive) disapproval for the things you don't. I call this setting the boundaries. I would add that you will need to ensure that your dog is fully vaccinated before allowing it to meet and engage with other dogs.

Once your dog hits the 5-8 month mark it will start challenging and exploring more independently and that's where the real fun starts! This period is 'doggy adolescence' and both a secondary exploration period (of self and environment) coming right on the heels of the start of its first fear stage (at circa 12 -15 weeks). A dog's 'fear stage' is where a dog sees new things/situations as no longer as readily accepted as they once were but instead treated with caution and suspicion by default.

In this 'adolescence' period, they may also be a bit more defiant and challenging. It is crucial therefore, that you maintain the consistency and training of rules and boundaries as, without direct guidance from you, your dog will internalise its own set of rules and act accordingly. It is often a very challenging time for you and your dog but if you stay focused and consistent then you both will get through this period stronger, wiser and more bonded.

At this point I would like to dispel a myth about calculating a dog's age. The long-held view is that 1 human year equates to 7 dog years but that is not always the case. The average human currently lives to about 85 years. If you use this as your marker then you should measure this directly against the average life span for the type of dog you have. You will be able to get the average life span expectations for your dog's breed on the internet. To calculate how old your dog is in human years divide the average human life span (85) with your dog's average life span. For example, if you have a Yorkshire Terrier then you would expect it to live between 12-15 years. Taking the top end of 15 years then the calculation would be 85/15 which equals 5.7 dog years for every human year, conversely if you have a Saluki, which is noted as having an average life span of 12 years then this calculation would result in the archetypal 7 dog years for every 1 human year.

The above being said, apart from anthropomorphising a dog's age, then it really gives little real value other than that. The real information to understand is the growth stages of a dog. I have noted below a quick generic overview on this. However, it is important to note that larger dogs will physically, but not necessarily mentally, grow and develop at a slower pace than small to medium dogs.

At approximately 6 months of age a dog will reach sexual maturity with reproductive maturity occurring between 6 to 9 months. Small to medium dogs will achieve structural maturity at about 9 months of age with larger dogs doing so between 12 – 18 months of age. Adulthood will be achieved at about 12 months of age with adult maturity (middle age) happening between 6 to 9 years. The senior years will begin from 9 years and any dog over 13 will enter its geriatric stage.

It is interesting to note that although smaller and larger dogs will physically develop at significantly different rates but there is not as distinct a difference when it comes to psychological development. For most dogs the crucial imprinting period goes from 0 to 12/14 weeks and this is the time that your dog's brain will develop and become hard wired in direct relation to the early experiences it is exposed to. We tend to get our new puppy at around 8 weeks therefore it is vital that we continue its education.

As the new 'mum' it is down to you to educate your canine charge and believe me you reap what you sow. If your pup does not experience all that life has to throw at it at an early stage of life then issues are likely to develop as the dog gets older and comes across a 'new' issue that it does not know how to deal with. It was Aristotle that said "give me the boy (child) until the age of seven and I will show you the man (adult)" and the principles are the same for dogs although you have to change seven years to seven months.

In addition, early negative experiences can develop into forms of fear aggression, phobias or other negative behavioural issues. However, this does not mean that you can just throw our pup into the middle of things and let them figure things out. Of course, you could do this and see how things turn out (they call this 'flooding' or "immersion") but you will have little control or influence on how well your dog adapts and is not something I would ever recommend and is likely to do more harm than good.

Remember, you are your pup's protector and I would want you to be seen as such by your pup ensuring that you place your fur ball into as few overly stressful situations as possible. You cannot always get it right of course but if you quickly, calmly and decisively respond when you see your dog getting stressed and looking for help then you will maintain the trust and positive relationship with it. Just to reinforce my thoughts here if, at any time, you think your dog is looking for you to help, especially when it could be frightened of some dog or something, then give it no questions asked. You are your dog's protector and you need to protect your dog. If a dog has to make these type of 'survival/threat' decisions itself then trust in you as a protector will be weakened significantly, if not lost altogether and trust is crucial in the bonding process.

I also believe dogs that have been thrown in at the 'deep end' will create a trauma events which, inevitably, will lead to a negative experience and possible (probable) behavioural issues, immediately, or at some point down the road. PTSD anyone? Yes, dogs can, ad do, suffer from Post Traumatic Stress Disorder (PTSD). I will go into more detail on this later in the book.

Personally, I like to be the teacher and retain control and guide my dog in the new experiences, especially socialisation, and I would guess so do you. I will go into more detail on how best to socialise your dog later in this book as well as busting a few socialisation myths.

As a general point in establishing acceptable behaviours and standards, it is important to start as you mean to go on. If you don't want your dog jumping up on you, or the furniture, then don't allow it from the start. It may be fun and cute when they are still a pup but they grow fast and basically you should not allow something as a pup that you do not wish to happen when your dog gets bigger.

Changing the rules mid-term is always a bad idea and will confuse your dog therefore it is better to set out the rules from the start and they will become embedded easier and quicker and become part of its framework for life. Your dog will not view itself as small and cuddly it will just accept that what it does is okay unless it receives feedback to the contrary. So please start as you mean to go on and give the correct guidance to your dog from the outset and you will definitely reap the benefits as it grows into an adult dog.

As previously stated, as dogs go from being a puppy to becoming an 'adult' dog they go through a 'fear stage' or, in some cases, a couple of fear stages between the ages of 4 – 12 months. This is where negative experiences have most chance to create negative reactions (trauma events) in your dog and often the most testing time for owners and dogs.

If this is already the case and your dog is already in the 'trouble zone' then the chapter on common issues and challenging behaviour will give you the tools to understand how best to re-educate your dog into more acceptable behaviours. In that chapter, you will not only be given some solutions to some common issues but you will also gain an understanding of the principles of why your dog reacts in the way it does. You will learn to view these situations from a dog's perspective and be able to communicate the changes you are looking for in a language it will understand.

Remember, an issue will not get any better if not addressed but it is likely to get worse!

By using the principles and tips in this book you will be setting expectations and basic rules (boundaries) with your dog even if you are not aware of doing so. Dogs live by simple rules and create 'desire' and 'coping' strategies relevant to its, immediate and foreseen, environment perceptions (survival resonance). For a dog this is core to its security and survival. Everything in a dog's world comes with a 'survival value' whether the object is living or inanimate.

However, as Alexander Horowitz notes in his book 'Inside of a Dog: What Dogs See, Smell and Know', that "with humans we never let one person's behaviour stand for all behaviour" and the same applies for dogs. Two dogs of the same breed and age that are displaying similar behavioural issues may have different reasons (motivators) for doing so. We cannot treat all dogs the same even if they are the same breed.

This book should serve as a toolkit designed to give you baseline references, ideas and tips in order for you to shape as required. That, being said, we do need to understand the primal thinking of a dog of 'positive', 'negative' and 'neutral'. This does not mean that dogs are not intelligent, far from it, but they do operate on a very simple satisfaction and protection model of reasoning. I have called this the dog's 'survival value'.

There are three survival values that shape the dog's view of the world. These values are as follows:-

Positive: I like it, I want it (or I want more of it) (food, comfort, safety (security), fun, sex).

Negative: I don't like it and I want less of it and/or away from it.

Neutral: It currently holds no positive or negative value but I know it is there and it is on the watch list. *It is important to note here that although noted as neutral it is probably more accurate to classify this as dormant as, in actuality, nothing, no matter how insignificant it seems to us, to a dog nothing is neutral. Any dog with OCD will tell you that. As a clear example of this one of my dogs (Darcy), who does display signs of autism to be fair, suddenly became reactive and suspicious one time when we had changed the curtains in the living room. After a while she learned to 'accept' the new curtains, and the change, and move on but it did 'spook' her initially.*

If you are familiar with (human) psychology you will see that the above is not quite the Maslow's Hierarchy of Needs (which are *Physiological Needs, Safety Needs, Belonginess & Love Needs, Esteem Needs and Need for Self-Actualization*). Dogs needs have far simpler (primal) needs. Although, in saying this, Linda Michaels

MA, has created a Hierarchy of Dog's Needs (HDN) similar to Maslow's (which is listed as *Biological Needs, Emotional Needs, Social Needs, Force Free Training Needs and Cognitive Needs*). These 'needs' align themselves with the previously stated primal principles of 'survival value' and is the gateway, in our dogs mind, to acceptance, suspicion or rejection to things, people, dogs and, of course, environments.

Also, as indicated previously, it is important to emphasise that everything, yes everything, that a dog sees, or comes into contact with, from people to curtains, has a survival value (positive, Negative or Neutral (dormant)) and a dog will assess and react accordingly.

So, let's start with the premise that dogs want immediate satisfaction as a default setting (which is always the case). Couple that with the fact that you want to be the provider of that satisfaction then you can call this 'foundation understanding'. Everything from here in should relate back to this. Is the dog happy – are you happy? They both need to be yes for optimum harmony but equally you should accept that there may be bumps in the road (see chapter 'managing set backs') but as long as you are there to help and support your dog then the trust in you will not diminish.

Trust is absolutely crucial in order to engage with and guide our dog as without this your dog will not always readily accept your direction. The receptivity of your input to your dog will be conditional on other (dog's internalised) survival factors such as clarity and consistency. If you, or those around you, are inconsistent with interactions and instruction then not only will this confuse your dog but it will learn to trust its own inner instinct more than it will trust the guidance from you and as a result it will become erratic in its response and reactions and, thus, unreliable.

Even feeding time should come with rules. I cannot underestimate how important eating is in a dog's world. Food is such a valuable resource and, for most dogs, a key driver to behavioural displays albeit good or bad. If you reward a dog when it is good it will tend to repeat this behaviour and continue to be good. However, if you reward your dog with food no matter the behaviour then the behaviour given will be set by the dog and not by you and you will lose control. This is one of the key reasons why you should set rules even for meal times.

In order to establish yourself as the resource giver I would recommend keeping to set times when issuing food, which will also help regulate your dog's toileting routine. In addition, I would not leave the food out for any longer than 15 minutes if your dog is not attending to it. Note, I would never recommend taking away your dog's food whilst it is eating nor would I advocate doing so with anything that your dog is actively engaged with. Removing the food after 15 minutes sets the rule with your dog that set meal times are exactly that, and, if it wants to eat, it needs to do so within this window. Don't worry, your dog will not go hungry or starve itself, as I say, food is a very valuable resource to a dog so it will maximise this opportunity. When removing the food however, I would not draw attention to this and aim to remove it silently and quickly. I would also, if you have removed an earlier meal, not look to pad out the next meal with the missed portion.

As I say, a dog will not starve, or go hungry, but it is important that you are seen as the resource provider and you will provide such within a set framework of rules. This will provide comfort to your dog as it will learn the routine and become secure in the fact knows when its next meal is coming and the window of time it has in which to eat it. Although, as an exception, to ensure adequate hydration, I would recommend leaving water out for your dog to access when it wishes but maintain set rules and access times for food and treats.

Communicating with your dog

How you deliver any communication is crucial. Dogs are very perceptive and not only listen to what you say and how you say it but they also 'read' the energy within the 'delivery' of the communication and, from this, either accepts or rejects it.

Let's be clear, what you say (words) is for your benefit not your dog's. Dogs are action orientated. To a dog, for an instruction to be readily accepted then the sound, vision and energy combined need to be collectively congruent. If anything seems out of sync to your dog then you may be inadvertently giving your dog a mixed message which may confuse it. Added to this is the dog's previous experiences of similar communication and outcomes will shape how your dog will interpret and react to the message in keeping with its own survival values.

As communication is so important I have broken down the 5 key elements for optimum delivery of <u>any</u> communication to your dog. I have called this the 5 Cs. The 5 Cs are a method of instruction delivery that will resonate with your dog and allow it, if done well, to trust in you almost unconditionally. The 5 Cs are Calm, Confident, Controlled, Consistent and Concise. I will now break this down and explain why this communication style is so effective for dogs.

Calm: Calmness resonates superbly well with dogs as it allows them to focus on <u>the message you wish to deliver</u> rather than the energy or emotion of the delivery which can, especially if it is high, be viewed as an 'alert' cue. A calm leader is one to be listened to. This is as true for humans as it is for dogs. This is especially crucial if you have a pessimistic dog as they will look to mirror their guardian by default due to the lack of internal confidence that they have in themselves.

High energy from you begets a high energy dog!

Note: All puppies are permanent high energy but this can be 'shaped' as they grow and develop into more balanced energy via the 5 Cs.

Confident: In order to ensure that your dog wholly trusts in you and does not try to fill in the gaps itself then you need to be confident and assured in the delivery of your message. Even if you don't feel confident. This gives your dog the security that you have everything in hand and that it does not need to worry about anything. You should be the protector of your dog and not vice versa. Once your dog understands this it will take guidance from you more readily and willingly.

Controlled: The key here is for your dog not to think but to do. For this to be achieved you need to ensure that your body language is definitive, matches your verbal language and that your energy is in keeping with being calm and confident. If not, then the instruction you are trying to deliver will be incongruent and your dog will pick up on this and treat your instruction with caution and suspicion. Dogs are very, very perceptive and always assess the whole picture to ensure that sound, sight and feel (energy) are consistent with their expectations.

Consistent: Although dogs are context based, whereby they can, in some cases, internalise different rules for different people, for best results they need to understand that there are no exceptions, whatsoever, to ensure that there is no confusion in what is required or expected. If you occasionally allow something to happen that you normally would not or constantly change the rules then you cannot blame your dog if it misbehaves because, in its mind, the rules of engagement are flexible.

Concise: Verbal and visual information should always be clear and easily distinguishable from other (background) sights and sounds. This is especially important when in training mode. Information (both visual and verbal) that is clear and concise will always stand the best chance of being 'received' by your dog and being (correctly) acted upon. Verbal chatter is commonplace for us humans but not so much for our dogs. If you want a certain outcome from your dog it is important that you 'talk with purpose' and remove superfluous sounds from your interactions with your dog.

If you adopt and use the 5 Cs then you should be able to guide and help your dog adapt to this strange and crazy world. Within the 5 Cs **consistency** is key and I have underlined this element due to its importance. Even if the message we give to our dog is the same but the style of delivery differs then there is absolutely no guarantee that our dog will understand, accept and/or interpret this correctly.

As noted previously, you are now the teacher. Now we know, from our own school days, that 'teacher' and 'fun' are not always comfortable bedfellows, rarely coupled together and, for many, seen as contradictory. But, that being said, we all had that one teacher who stood out, who was totally there for us and inspired us to learn more than we would have done so under normal circumstances. To get the best results you need to be that 'inspiring' teacher else it is going to be a long and tortuous journey for both you and your dog. You may still get the end results you crave but you would have done it the hard way and, I would guess, you had to revert to the style of a Drill Sergeant barking instructions more times than you would care to remember. I am not a fan of authoritarianism and I suspect neither is your dog.

As an example of this, I remember, a few years back now, taking my eldest son to soccer training which was run by a chap called Ian Dool, who has, sadly, since died. Ian knew how to command respect. Now to create some context this soccer club was not in the salubrious part of Glasgow in Scotland but instead housed squarely in a much-deprived area with little in the way of facilities or support. Somehow though, this team were regular league champions and I thought it would be a good fit for my son who was showing some early signs of talent on the soccer field. He was successful in the trial and subsequently joined the club.

Therein, over the weeks and months, I became awestruck at the command and control Mr Dool had with these kids many of whom came from very troubled backgrounds and held little, if any, respect for any type of authority. Using 'Dool's Rules' the kids done everything that was asked of them and then some. They gave the proverbial 110% for him. I was so impressed, and I am not an easy man to impress, that I joined the team as a coach and trained for my coaching certificates just because 'I' wanted to be part of his team.

Now Ian was not a big man, in fact he was quite small and even smaller than me and I am about the size of an 'Action Man' figure. He was not loud and he was not bullish. No, he was charismatic, receptive and funny but, more importantly, he was consistent, focused and motived on achieving success. Success was not about winning leagues, although that did happen, but ensuring that the kids were motivated to turn up, train, learn and maximise their potential no matter where they ranked in the team.

It was a great balance of fun and rules (Dool's Rules) with a real working together ethic. It was a true partnership approach. If Ian liked what you had done he would let you know which encouraged you to do the same again. If he did not like what you had done he would tell you but equally, at the same time, he would 'teach' you what he did like. There was no talking down, shouting, pointing fingers or making examples of anyone, no matter the issue. In addition, everything was interlaced with having fun which kept the kids interested and engaged. I have tried to maintain these ethics in my professional and personal life and I can testify to the successes of these principles.

As with Ian and the soccer team kids, I like to think that we are here to teach, guide and not bully our dogs into submission. This is why I adopt the positive reinforcement approach to training dogs.

Positive reinforcement (R+) training over 'old school' harsher (alpha) techniques gives me the consistently excellent results I have achieved to date. Yes, bullying your dog may get them to do what you want but the cost will be the trust and bond between you and your dog. In addition, they will not perform the action because they want to but rather because they 'have to' and will give you the bare minimum in order to escape punishment. You will be condemned to a lifetime of pushing like a Drill Sergeant rather than becoming a teacher or guide. I prefer to adopt the role of teacher rather than one of rank.

As a teacher you understand that to get best results you need motivated and focused students. The same is true for dog development. You need to be the centre of your dog's world during times of training and development. This means you need to manage energy and focus. It does not mean that you have to be super excited or high energy every time you want your dog's attention. I am not a super excitable 'always on' person but I know what energies to muster in order to get the best reaction from the dogs in my charge.

Coupled with the 5 Cs there are three further very simple rules for the optimum delivery of *initial* training; 1) No distractions; 2) Balanced energy; 3) Eyes on you. I have highlighted in bold 'initial' training as the aim is to be able to eventually get good training responses within distractive environments but initially it is best to conduct training in a distraction free environment. You will also look to build in distance and duration into your training program but, again, this should only happen when you are consistently getting the required responses when working close to your dog. As stated, in respect of rule one (distractions) can, and needs to be, added only once the behaviour you want is set-in and <u>consistently</u> displayed. However, introduce distraction too soon and you increase the difficulty of solidifying the desired response ten-fold.

Given **rule one** (no distractions) it is strange that we feel that taking our pup to puppy classes will be the best training platform for us when, in reality, it is far from ideal. Basically, puppy classes are good for social exposure and understanding the techniques to train but not ideal for initial training as there are too many distractions, too much down time, uncontrolled energies and you are surrounded by other untrained dogs!

The above being said, if you view the puppy classes as a forum to learn tips and ideas which you can take away to practice at home coupled whilst gaining experience of trying to teach your dog to focus on you amongst the bedlam then you will not go far wrong. You will get the best out of puppy classes if you don't put too much pressure on yourself, or your dog, to perform on the night as that is neither fair on you nor your dog. Remember you are trying to guide your dog within an uncontrolled and active environment and the best initial training should always be done within a controlled and inert environment.

A word of warning though, if, in puppy class, your pup shows signs of significant distress (straining towards to the door, whining/howling, hiding, cowering, nipping, snarling or biting etc) it may be best to revert to train privately and look to eventually and slowly reintroduce your pup to other dogs in less stressful situations. If your dog is making it clear that they are uncomfortable then as a good teacher you will listen to their feedback, take them to a place of comfort and rebuild. In the latter respect, always aim to build up confidence in your dog before you deploy exposure to training in a multi-dog environment and both you and your dog will positively benefit from this approach. Another thing to remember is that your dog is unlikely to be listening or focusing on you if it is preoccupied or stressed with everything else around therefore you will both be in for a very unproductive and unrewarding time if that is the case.

Rule two (Balanced Energy) is also vital in that you want your dog to be in training receptive mode and to get there they need to expend at lot of energy beforehand. Trying to train a dog who is like a coiled spring in terms of energy waiting to be released is somewhat challenging as their focus, and drive, will be all over the place. It is always best to let your dog run about, play fetch etc, for about 10-15 minutes or so before any training to burn off excess energy.

Remember though, puppies need plenty of rest so keep training sessions short and fun (5-10 minutes max).

Rule three (Eyes on You) is the catalyst for all things good and we need your dog to understand this. Therefore, you need to become the most exciting and rewarding thing in its world at that time and the giver of good things (treats, toys, praise).

Through continued positive experience with you then your dog will realise that time with you is fun and training is really just play with purpose. You are setting the interactions with you as being always positive therefore your dog will become more receptive and should continually look to you for guidance.

The best way to ensure this happens is by asking yourself "what reason am I giving Fido to focus on me?" and if you cannot think of a reason then, chances are, neither can your dog. However, don't worry too much if you don't get 100% eye contact initially as you can build this up but you do need your dog's desire to be with you otherwise everything else may become more interesting than you and you will have lost its attention and, more importantly, its focus.

You now have your foundation to deliver communication that resonates with your dog. You know that understanding a dog's survival values, communicating via the 5 Cs and setting the right conditions by adhering to the 3 rules of initial training will have the best chances of success.

The next key step is to understand that you are dealing with a dog. This may sound obvious but, believe it or not, many of the behavioural issues I deal with are down to the fact that the dog is treated like a human.

In general, people tend to talk too much and anthropomorphise reactions displayed by their furry friend. However, this is all counter-productive due to the fact that dogs don't really understand the world they live in and have limited ways to communicate back to us. Dogs need their guardians to set out their world in simple, yet structured ways. Also, dogs don't do exceptions therefore, again, you need to be consistent when it comes to your interactions and instructions.

Furthermore, you need to remove as much emotion as possible as dogs are very highly-tuned when it comes to reading energies (and emotion). Dogs also tend to amplify energy levels ten-fold which could be counter-productive and result in your dog to focusing on your energy (emotion) and not the message you are trying to give.

Remember, dogs think on a primal level therefore, for best results, you need to do likewise. Although dogs generally live in the moment they do build a series of experiences which are rated (conditioned) in one of three emotional banks of **Positive** (Pos) – I like it and want to experience more of it; **Negative** (Neg) – I don't like it and do not want to experience it again; **Neutral** (Neu) – it has no meaning to me therefore I discard any notice of it – for now but it is always on the watch list.

That's it. There are no anthropomorphic connotations that dogs adopt. It is as simple as 1, 2 or 3. You should not humanise a dog's response as by doing so you will fail to read your dog on a dog's level.

As an example, guilt and shame is often labelled against a dog when it has been identified as the culprit of some unwanted behaviour or destruction and challenged for such. e.g. "I came home and the place was a riot. I looked at Fido and his head was down and he looked guilty as hell". Eh, no. What he has more likely done is made a quick assessment of your body language, facial expression, vocals (tone, pitch, stress etc) and coupled this with similar previous experiences and concluded what is likely to follow is going to be negative (Neg) therefore he is lowering his head, looking away and making himself small in order to protect himself (survival) against any negative impact. This is natural appeasement behaviour.

If you can maintain a primal view of dog actions then this will help you greatly when trying to decode your dog.

You now understand how best to communicate with your dog and how your dog will receive (understand) these 'messages'. Add to this the environment, which is everything that is surrounding it, and you will begin to understand what all this means in relation to a dog's perceived 'survival resonance'.

I would note here that although I have titled this book "Decode Your Dog" in reality, as with the poker analogy, the dog has to decode us also and we then have to decode its reactions to us, our energy, emotion and the environment, in order to achieve true communication connection. That being said, you can now do this with confidence knowing what resonates with your dog. This understanding is key and, in the chapter, "Putting it all Together" we will look at how best you can apply this knowledge.

'HOW DOGS LEARN' CHAPTER SUMMARY

- Dog observation exercise
- Dog senses
- Coprophagia
- Scent marking
- Living in the moment
- Being Mum
- Learning life's rules
- Setting standards
- Addressing behaviour
- Rebellious period and fear stage
- Addressing behaviour
- Survival values
- Immediate satisfaction drive
- Foundation Understanding
- Communicating via the 5 Cs
- Being the good teacher
- 3 rules of initial training

Chapter 3: Putting it all Together

As in chapter 2 this chapter will give you further insight into what works best for your dog when trying to train or develop them by tying everything together.

Before I begin, I would like to address two of the common questions I get asked generally and when conducting consultations. These are "when can I start training?" and "how long will it take?". The first question is an easy one to answer. The day you get your dog is the day training should begin. A dog is never too young to learn and is already predisposed to learning and adapting. Conversely a dog is never too old to learn. You can, and should, teach an older dog new tricks.

The second question is more challenging to answer as it depends on so many factors such as the training starting point, the training objectives, the time and commitment you can invest, the training delivery style and the training environment. You can then add to this the dog's history, breed, temperament, health etc and you can see that providing a time scale is, very often, a finger in the air exercise. However, as learning should start from day one then it should only end when your dog is unable, due to health, to perform what is required. Training is a lifetime commitment and a life choice. As it is the case with people, we are learning, adapting and changing all of the time, then so it should be with our dogs. Dogs love interacting with us and dogs love learning. Why would you ever want that to end?

By all means, phase out the treats and the other short term 'incentives' and move onto praise (with occasional treat/toy rewards) but don't stop the training. Again, as it is with people, if you are taught and learn something that you eventually become good at, your performance of this skill will only stay competent if you maintain practice. Of course, the more you practice the more proficient you become. It is exactly the same for dogs. So, understanding this, how do you put it all together?

You know that dogs are expert observers, you know they are predisposed to adapt, you know that they think on a primal level and you know that they act for the moment they are in. What you will learn in this chapter is what they do with the information you communicate to them and how you can use this knowledge to help train and/or develop your dog.

Dogs are hard wired to please and are bred to be social animals. In fact, interacting with humans is so hard wired that by interacting with us it releases dopamine (the pleasure chemical) into the dog. This makes them ideal candidates for training and development. We, as humans, just need to understand what they are telling us and communicate to them in ways that make sense for them.

In this chapter you will learn the methodologies of intuitive communication, the structured mechanics of training and what this means for your dog and how this can achieve amazing results. It may sound complicated but it really isn't.

Before you begin any training you need to ensure that your dog is ready to be trained. This means that you need to give it the opportunity to expel some excess energy before you ask it to focus on you. You can do this via a 10-15 minute high energy game or exercise such as fetch, raggy, go hunt etc. I will expand on games in the 'its playtime' chapter. An exercised dog with much of its excess physical energy spent will be in the ideal mental state for training. Ideally, you are looking for a game or exercise that burns both mental and physical energy.

Mental energy is argued by many dog professionals, as being more exhausting for a dog than physical energy as many dogs can run for hours and still have room in the tank for more. I very much support this train of thought as I have found that the dogs I work with seem to sleep longer, sounder and very soon after completing training or brain games. Some dogs you could walk for miles and they are just getting started but then you give them a few mental challenges and they are soon dead to the world.

Note: It is important not to over-exercise your dog, especially puppies, therefore the 5 - 10 minutes of vigorous exercise before training should be enough for most dogs.

To get the best out of training the sessions should be short anyway (again no longer than 10 – 15 minutes in duration) but, ideally, frequent (2 - 4 times) during the day. Taking matters from a primal perspective most dogs have short attention spans and couple this with ADHD, which most dogs seem to have, then it pays to keep things short, fun and regular.

Breed may have an influence on learning styles of course and working dogs will require more sustained training and development. However, as stated at the outset this book is not designed for the 'working dog' even though I believe the principles stated in this book will work, in general, across all breeds and job roles. If your dog is clearly showing an appetite to continue then by all means continue – you are the best gauge of how long to keep things going with your dog. It is always recommended to leave your dog wanting more therefore guaranteeing full engagement when you recommence the training program later on.

So, with all of this in mind you need to put together a structured training and development plan. For you to be able to do this I need to deconstruct what training actually means to us and our dogs.

The aim of training is to issue a command (instruction) and for your dog to respond accordingly. When this happens successfully a reward is given thus increasing the likelihood of it being repeated in the future. This may seem obvious but for this to work effectively there are four crucial components that all need to work well. I call this the four-step response cycle.

For us the four step response cycle on which <u>most of us</u> feel our dogs understand is made up of '**Command**' (the issuing of a directive request (hopefully using the 5 Cs technique)); '**Reaction**' (how our dog responds, if at all, to the instruction); '**Outcome**' (successful, not successful, or nil reaction) and '**Bank**' (what we learn (positive/negative) from the reaction). **In summary**: Command – Reaction – Outcome – Bank.

However, seeing the above from a dog's perspective then it will be '**Sound**' (hopefully distinctive and distinguishable as words mean little other than a sound); '**Action**' (Do I (dog) recognise this sound?; what should I do now?); '**Experience**' (was the previous reward for my response, if anything at all, good or bad?) and '**Bank**' (will I be motivated or demotivated to respond likewise, if at all, in the future). **In summary**: Sound – Action – Experience – Bank.

Visual signals are equally significant and should work in conjunction with, and be congruent with the sound/instruction given. It is also important to state that dogs can pick out words within our sentences and act accordingly but, for training, it is always more effective to keep everything clear and distinct in order to avoid confusion and misinterpretations arising and to ensure that your dog is actually responding to the correct word and not, inadvertently, another word in the command sentence.

You can see from the above that the delivery of an instruction (command) results in two different four step response cycles. One response cycle is from our perspective and the latter is from the dog's. This is an important differentiation that understanding such will help get the best results within the shortest amount of time with your dog. You then need to work on their level and to their agenda accepting that most of what you ask your dog to do is unnatural for it. Given this you need to incentivise your dog in order for it to successfully adopt your instruction and comply. You can do this by understanding their four-step response cycle over ours.

Dog chat

We know dogs do talk (growling, barking) but, in my experience, this is often done for one of the four reasons noted below and it is not done to instruct or issue commands: -

1. They are warning you of something (noise, stranger, intruder etc)
2. They are excited/frustrated (energy release - often higher pitched barking)
3. They want something (including your attention on them)
4. They want something to go away/anxiety (growling and/or barking)

I remember, attending a workshop on dog communication and it was stated that dogs do not vocalise to other dogs apart from when they are warning them away or warning of a desire to attack. I agree that dogs do tend to act rather than request more often than not but I don't agree with the premise that dogs generally don't bark at each other. In my experience, dogs do bark at each other much for the same four reasons noted above as they do to humans. Once you understand the above then you should accept and welcome vocal feedback as it is giving you information on your dog's state of mind. If a dog is not allowed to vocalise then it will likely go straight to 'action', which is certainly not desirable and can have potentially horrendous consequences.

It is prudent to note that it is not barking per se that is the problem but moreover excessive barking that is the issue for many dogs. I will cover how to deal with excessive barking in the chapter "Common Issues and Challenging Behaviour".

Now you have our communication baseline you can start to plan your training programs knowing that you are talking and directing in the way your dog has the best chance of understanding. However, you now need to condition your dog in order to respond in the desired way(s). This is done by allowing your dog to make, hopefully correct, choices or to activate automatic responses to sounds or other stimulus it experiences. These are called conditioned responses and these underpin positive reinforcement dog training and development.

I had stated at the outset of this book that I did not want to write a jargon laden book, but it is important that I give you a brief overview of the two conditioning types which are 'classical conditioning' and 'operant conditioning'.

Classical conditioning (coined by Ivan Pavlov) is where the subject, in this case a dog, instinctively reacts to a trigger (visual or audio stimuli) in a way that they cannot control. For example, a dog starts salivating when it hears a bell as when it heard the sound of the bell previously a reward followed shortly thereafter. Because of this, its brain is now programmed to expect the same again. This response bypasses logical thinking in the dog and triggers an automatic (automotive) response.

Operant conditioning however is where a decision process (choice) actually takes place and the subject (dog) responds in a certain way based on a perceived outcome. An example of this would be that your dog chooses to come over to you when you call it as it knows, based on previous experience, that it will receive praise, or a treat, for doing so. The dog is (hopefully) incentivised to make the choice on how to respond.

Given the above you now understand that a dog will either respond automatically (classically conditioned) or make a choice based on perceived outcomes (operant conditioned). Positive reinforcement training uses both operant and classical conditioning. Basically, you are allowing your dog to learn through experience and reward.

The key to successful training and behaviour development is how you reward desired or punish undesired 'responses' from your dog. Basically, you should want to support your dog in making desired choices and discourage your dog from making undesired choices.

Old school methods such as being the 'alpha' and being dominant over your dog do not really allow the dog 'free choice' and work on the principle of consequence avoidance. These may get results but will achieve such for the wrong reasons and you will be condemned to always having to boss your dog forever and a day to get it to comply. In my opinion, it is bullying your dog into a compliant state rather than allowing it to learn and build a desire to perform preferred behaviours.

By focusing on 'correct choice' rewarding should mean that any rewards received by your dog will encourage (reinforce) your dog to do more of the same which, let's be honest, can only be a good thing. However, any punishment given should deter negative reactions from being repeated. Note that I have stated "will" for the reward and "should" for the punishment. I have done so on purpose.

You see whilst dogs readily accept the good things in life such as praise, toys or treats etc but when it comes to punishment things are not so straightforward. There is good reason for this. Enjoying the good things in life is a 'no-brainer' quite literally. These rewards bypass all thinking mechanisms in a dog and it will, assuming no behavioural, stress or confidence issues, just accept the joy to be had. When it comes to punishments though this is a different game and a whole lot of thinking goes on.

Thinking primal, when we, as humans, get good things rarely does anything bad also happen therefore we tend to be acceptive and care-free of such. Transpose this into a survival element and we can clearly postulate that 'good things' give us a positive reward value and therefore we don't need to think about anything other than how can we get more of it. It is the same for dogs but with the exception that, after training, they know they can only obtain the reward by responding in the way they (perceive) you want in order to initiate release of the reward. It is welcome and wanted. Not too much thinking required.

When it comes to punishments then we can safely assume to your dog these are neither welcome nor wanted. Punishments fall directly into the negative survival value and unlock a dog's primal defence response which has the core objective of how to avoid this punishment (immediately) and, if necessary, again in the future. Instantly, this raises the 'tread with caution' mental state in the dog with avoidance being its default position.

Avoidance will be the 'go to' position for most dogs assuming, of course, no mental or physical health issues where their 'reaction' may be governed more by pain or fear reactivity rather than survival logic. It is a phallacy that dogs are aggressive by default. Dogs, by default, tend not to engage with a threat unless they feel they have to. Instead most dogs will look to create distance from the danger as their default option. This is one of the main reasons why dogs are more reactive when on a lead as the option of 'flight' has been removed from it.

However, seeing punishments from a dog perspective it is not the action preceding the punishment that it will tend to focus on but the delivery of it. Dogs will, in all likelihood, go straight to baseline and look at the punisher as the reason for this negative reaction and on its own behaviour. By default, the dog will want to avoid the punisher...you!

Trust is replaced by fear and everything therein is treated with caution until confidence and trust has been rebuilt, if it indeed can be. It will not matter a jot if you had spent hours of cuddles and play beforehand once your dog feels the need to invoke this negative survival value everything you have done previously is placed into the 'proceed with caution' (negative) basket.

Trust is such a vital element in your dog's world. It really cannot be understated. If a dog trusts you it will listen to you and, if it listens to you, it will learn to rely on your judgement and guidance over its own. You will become the provider of not only food and lodging but also safety and security. Add to this lots of cuddles and play then you will give your dog no reason to internalise its own, self-referenced, survival rules. If the trust is strong then this will remove survival burden from your dog and thus the survival pressures.

Assuming your dog is healthy and happy it can still, in some dogs, take a while to build conditional or unconditional trust. I do state 'unconditional trust' but rarely is anything in a dog's world unconditional, for example, even with a dog you have worked hard to build trust with it may not take long at all to lose it. In fact, it can be pretty immediate, even in a dog that was previously pretty open and trusting. Dogs, even though they are bred to be social and live within domesticated environments, are survivalists.

If the above is all good then fun (positive reinforcement) training will be more effective because your dog will want to do things for you (a desire to please) because you will be providing enriching experiences and thus enhancing the emotional bond and positively motivating your dog's continued willingness to please. Not to mention releasing of all that wonderful dopamine!

Without trust you are going to have a very difficult and challenging time trying to get your dog to positively respond to you. If your dog is not fully embracing your interactions and looks to create distance at each opportunity that arises then I would focus on building positive experiences with you dog before you fully immerse yourself in any structured training at all. Remember all interactions with your dog are training opportunities even if there is no other goal but to engage, interact and play.

It is also important to note that it is not to say you cannot punish your dog because that is plainly ridiculous as you need to be able to show your dog your displeasure for inappropriate and potentially dangerous actions. However, you can do so via 'positive' means which neither destroy trust nor the relationship you have with your dog.

All dogs need boundaries and it is via teaching what is acceptable and not-acceptable that your dog will learn these boundaries. A further point on this is to ensure that you play happy when you are playing but ensure that you are calm and not angry when you are showing disapproval. Emotion is such a vital factor as it dictates how receptive your dog is likely to be to the message you are trying to convey. I will expand more on this later in the chapter 'common issues and challenging behaviour'.

Now onto chapter 4: Energy and Structured Training.

'PUTTING IT ALL TOGETHER' CHAPTER SUMMARY

- Dogs are social by default
- Exercised dog
- Issuing instructions
- How dogs interpret and act
- Dog chat
- Conditioned responses
- Rewarding choices
- Trust

Chapter 4: Energy and Structured Training

The last key point is energy. I know I am repeating myself but, again, this element is not to be understated. Energy equals frame of mind and focus. You need balanced energy and focus from both you and your dog otherwise you will not have the engaging experience that you need in order to guide your dog to success. If your dog is overly energised then it will need to expel this before you can even think of training. If not, you will be fighting for attention and focus from your dog at every step meaning that your guidance will not be 'received' as well as it should be.

I have also stated previously that mental energy is as important as physical energy. I would argue that mental energy, for many of the higher intelligent breeds such as Collie's etc, is of more importance than physical. Let's be honest, some dogs we can walk for miles and they have not even broken a sweat. There are few dogs that we will be able to out-walk. Given this we need to exercise them in other ways to ensure that they are adequately fulfilled. Far too often I see dogs that have some behavioural issues due in the main because they have little, or no, mental outlet. All dogs that crave mental stimulation which, unfortunately, if it does not receive it will start to satisfy itself in other often more destructive or noisy ways.

If you have a dog, not a puppy, that you just cannot tire, even after lengthy walks, or you have a dog that is destructive it may be that your dog is looking for way to burn off its excess mental energy. This is often a cry for help. If you don't act then the negative behaviours will not get better and are likely to get worse and could, if not addressed, turn into 'learned' or even 'OCD' behaviours.

Now, the best way to manage a dog's energy is not to raise ours or expose our dog to high energy environments/people/dogs until it is able to perform its own energy self-control. We, as guardians, should lead by example and in a calm, assertive and non-emotive state as possible. Dogs are generally a good mirror to their environment and lifestyle.

You should also take great care to remember your dog is a dog and not a furry human. If you have a tendency to 'baby' your dog and smother it with attention then it will not learn to be a dog, which is vital, and will become over-reliant on you to provide all of the answers. A needy dog, who is overly reliant on you and unable, or unwilling, to work things out for itself, will always be a needy dog and will never progress unless we give it the time, space and support to do so. This is 'learned helplessness' and is not conducive to producing a healthy and happy dog but, instead, often produces a stressed and nervous dog.

In addition, a dog that is pampered can easily become a spoilt dog, which, in my opinion, is worse than a spoilt kid as you can always 'talk to the kid', even if they don't listen, but cannot do so as much with your dog and the consequences of something going wrong can be catastrophic. Further, if a dog has no experience of making its own choices it will have no confidence in dealing with issues therefore will naturally be wary of everything unless you are there to hold its paw. This can be overly stressful for a dog. Dogs take great comfort from great leadership and this will not only increase its own confidence but also the trust and bond it will have with you. With all this in mind let's look at managing energy in your dog.

1. **Low and slow**

   If your dog is 'always on' or 'energy reactive (where their energies increase as quick as turning on a light)' then you need to teach them that good things happen when the brakes are applied. You also need to give any rewards or praise from the ground up and not from the top down. When your dog's head is lowered its energies will also lower. It is also wise to stroke, cuddle or pat your dog in slow deliberate movements and not accompanied by any chat. This will give your dog the comfort you wish to give but without the energy it can feed off.

   To achieve this, you need to ensure that your energies are low in the first place and it will also help to moderate your tone to almost monotone level. The aim here is to remove any, covert or overt, elements that may inadvertently excite your dog. In this respect, if your dog is in a highly excitable state then, if you can and if it is safe to do so, wait it out. Your dog will need to pause for breath. At that point you can issue the word "calm" (or similar) and slowly introduce a treat (from underneath its head/nose) whilst gently placing your hand (not moving) on the back of its neck and issue some quiet praise. If your dog resumes its high energy then stop and, again, wait it out.

You will now be rewarding your dog for calmness. If things go 'high energy' again and your dog chooses to amp things up then you should break the contact again and restart the process. If you maintain all interactions with your dog in a 'low and slow' manner your dog will become attuned to being rewarded for calmness and will eventually adopt these principles as the norm. Your dog will eventually get it especially if you use the 5 Cs in all communication displaying constant calm and assertive energies.

2. **Manage the environment**

This aspect can be super-tough to achieve but it really pays dividends if you can. Young children running around a dog can raise a dog's energies to astronomical levels. Another common issue is the frequency of guests coming and going from the home. To combat this you need to set some rules to be applied around your dog. The rules are simple – no interaction, from anyone coming or going, with your dog until it is in a calm state. Once your dog is calm then it can be called over and instructed to sit (or lie down) and then, only then, can the fun interactions begin. This will teach your dog that it does not have uncontrolled access to the energy feed and that it also needs 'to give something to get something' (a sit in exchange for praise, cuddles etc). Your dog will also learn to focus on the instruction(s) given because, now, this is the gateway to the fun and interaction. If this is in place your dog will learn boundaries and to moderate its behaviour accordingly.

3. Impulse control

As noted in 'game 2' (later in the book) impulse control is a great activity in order to help build self-control and restraint in your dog as well as reinforcing you as the resource provider. Impulse control is not only a great activity for energy management and defining boundaries and it also helps in overcoming so many behavioural issues. For me, teaching a dog impulse control should be one of the first things all owners should do as the benefits of this are so great.

4. Burn the energy off

This may seem a bit counter-intuitive but high energy games are great ways to start the day and help expel excess energy your dog may have. You may only have to play a game for 10-15 minutes to burn off the excess energy in your dog. Here are 5 high-energy games you could play: -

1. Play Fetch

As noted in 'game 3' (again later in the book) playing fetch is a great way to burn off excess energy whilst rewarding your dog with some fun play.

2. *Flirt Pole*

   Dogs that like to chase things will love the 'flirt pole' whereby a soft/fluffy object is tied to a pole via some string. These are easy to make but can also be purchased in your local pet store. 10 minutes vigorously chasing the furry toy will often be enough to satisfy most dogs, especially the smaller 'terrier' breeds or sight hounds.

3. *Home agility*

   If you have the space in your garden then why not build some obstacles for your dog to jump over or you can purchase play agility kits that include hurdles, weave poles, tunnels etc.

4. *Add Some Weight to carry*

   Why not consider giving your dog a job and put a back pack on it and get it to carry water bottles, poo bags etc. You will be surprised how much more energy is burned on a 15 to 20 minute walk when carrying a full, of nearly full, back pack as opposed to when it is not. Please make sure that the back pack is not too heavy for your dog and should always be near-empty (or only carry light things such as poo bags) for pups and small dogs.

5. *Add some weight to pull*

   It will go without saying that husky type dogs will love to pull things but it is not exclusively a husky activity. Assuming your dog is of the size and stature that it can pull some weight without placing strain on it then this could be a good solution to burning off energy.

   The above being said, this is a marmite activity whereby some dogs will love this activity and some dogs will not like it at all and, if that is the case, will not move. If this appeals to your dog then this can be a great energy burn-off as well as a good bonding activity also. If not, then just look to one of the other activities noted here.

   Two things of importance to note for this activity is to ensure that the weight to be pulled is not overly burdensome. You want the resistance to be evident but not restrictive. If your dog struggles to move off with the weight attached then this will mean that the weight is too much. The weight does not need to be, nor should be, labour-some, as the excess energy will be spent anyway, even pulling a relatively light weight.

The other important thing to note is to ensure is that you get a good sturdy and well-fitting harness where the weight is spread across the chest and not the neck or back.

Again, this is not a recommended activity for puppies or small dogs.

5. Join a club

Joining a local agility, flyball, cani-cross or similar type of 'dog activity' club is a great avenue for both owner and dog. These clubs not only afford great structured learning to occur but does so within a multi-dog and multi-distractive environments. Your dog will not only learn to focus on instruction within such an environment but will do so whilst also having a great time. This may seem at odds with the advice on training in a non-distracted environment but it really isn't as the activity itself' is the training and not the command/instruction from you. The mental and physical energy that is spent in these type of doggy clubs is almost beyond measure. At the end of each session you should have a tired, yet satisfied dog.

The last point of note on this subject is it should not all be school, school, school. Free play, where your dog is given time to do its own thing, be goofy, sniff until there is no tomorrow, run around daft (zoomies) etc is of equal importance to the actual training itself. Your dog will need the time to decompress and burn energy without having to worry about listening to instructions. Remember that all work and no play made Jack a very dull boy. Neither you, nor your dog, should become Jack and 'downtime', 'fun-time' should very much be part of the curriculum.

Leadership and Control

In your dog's eyes, you provide the food, lodging, safety, security, energy and emotion. From this, if consistent and balanced, your dog will trust in your leadership and guidance, especially if you use the 5 Cs, and you will have an engaged, confident and content dog. This, for me, is the absolute foundation in order to optimise any, and all, training and development potential.

In order to effectively guide your dog you will need to look at appropriate reinforcement and punishment. Don't worry about the word punishment as this does not mean anything punitive but, instead, reflective breaks, whereby you are not rewarding behaviours that you do not want to see.

There are two types of reinforcement and two types of punishment. It is good to know these differences but it is not a requirement to remember (this is not an academic book and there is not test at the end). The two types of reinforcement are: -

Positive reinforcement: This is where you give something (i.e. a treat, praise etc) as a marker letting your dog know it has done well and rewarding it for doing so. This should strengthen the chances of the desired behaviour being repeated again in the future by your dog.

Negative reinforcement: This is where you remove/take away something unpleasant to your dog (i.e. you stop raising your voice or shouting). The aim here is to 'reward' your dog's response by removing the unpleasant 'thing' in order to, hopefully, strengthen the desired behaviour in your dog. Note: I would never recommend, or support, shouting at your dog (see the 5 Cs) unless in an emergency situation such as to stop it running onto a road etc.

The two types of punishment are pretty much the same in respect of positive and negative. These are explained as: -

Positive Punishment: A positive punishment is where you introduce something (i.e. a slap, a sharp lead correction (pull) etc) in order to reprimand and/or 'correct' your dog. **Note**: I would NEVER support any physical reprimand of a dog and, if I need to physically redirect my dog, I tend to guide it rather than push or pull it. Dog's do not receive force well and tend to react to force with force or, at the very least, extra stubbornness.

Negative Punishment: This is where you remove something that your dog wants (i.e. food, toy, attention etc) as a punitive measure. Note: I would NEVER recommend taking anything from your dog (i.e. food, toy etc) if it is still engaged with it unless, of course, it is likely to cause it harm and, even then if you can, trade (swap the undesired item with something more appropriate) rather than take.

Now that we understand this, we can start to build a training structure.

In order to build a good training structure, you need to set up a good reward system. I like to initially set up (classically condition) an automatic response cue for the dog, as a way of saying to it "well done", which I can trigger when required. What I mean by this is that you can build an association of a <u>sound</u> (marker), for example I say "great or okay etc", with a (perceived) reward, such as a high value treat.

For best results, you should practice emitting the sound (marker) and giving your dog the high value reward until it gets to a point where your dog will automatically 'expect' (and 'look' for) that (high-level) reward automatically. This response bypasses your dog's decision making processes and becomes conditioned into an automatic response in your dog. I call this an auto-motive response. It is, in effect, classical conditioning where the dog automatically responds to the set sound with no decision process being apparent.

The marker (as coined in training circles) is a distinct sound that the dog will react to automatically without any thought or hesitation. This sound needs to be short, clear and distinct for best results and also to avoid confusion in your dog. Many trainers use a clicker but I tend to use the word 'okay' and it seems to work for me. There are no hard and fast rules on this and whatever works for you and your dog is all that matters.

In order to embed (classically condition) the reward expectation in your dog you need to build a positive association with the marker (sound) and a reward of some description (reinforcer). I use small treats for this but it could easily be a favourite toy or praise. However, the 'reward' needs to be of a high enough value (view this as 'dog' currency) for the dog to feel it is adequately rewarded for its efforts and, for me, treats do work best in this respect.

Now remember you are not training any activity here at all. All you are doing is establishing the relationship of the trigger sound (i.e. clicker sound, "okay", "yes" etc) to the reward by immediately rewarding the dog upon making the marker sound. Nothing else.

To effectively embed the response, you will need to do this lots and lots of times and you will need to do it over a number of days, if not weeks for some dogs, to ensure that the response is automatic and instinctive (classically conditioned). Once you see your dog responding consistently without any apparent hesitation then you have set your marker and auto-motive response. This can now be used as your reward (the yes this is correct, well done sound) for training.

It is important that during such intensive training you should reduce the portion sizes of their meals to compensate for the treats given and protect against over-feeding your dog. You can, if it still incentivises your dog, use some of your dog's dry food (if that what it gets fed) as training treats. Also, the actual treat size does not need to be big at all as it is the whole experience (treat, interaction and praise) that will act as the reward therefore even very small treats should be sufficient. That being said, as I will cover in more detail later in the book the value of the reward on offer needs to be sufficient in order to obtain the focus or response you are looking for in your dog. If you look at this as dog currency then sometimes you will need to pay $1 and other times $5 in order to get the desired response from your dog.

Okay, so we are now good to go? Well, nearly. To help consolidate the above I have compiled 8 simple rules to effective structured training which contain 3 'Golden' rules which should set you and your dog up nicely for success and not frustration and failure.

Rule #1:   **Keep commands to one or two syllables at most**. Phrases and sentences mean little to your dog so keep it short and simple. Dogs can, on occasion, pick out key words and short phrases from normal dialogue but it is best to keep things clear and simple for your dog to have the best chance of success.

Rule #2:   **Be mindful of your body language**. Be aware, as stated previously, dogs are expert observers. You may be issuing a command to do one thing but your dog does another because your dog may be linking an inadvertent hand, arm, head gesture etc to the alternative action.

In the communication priority of a dog the visual is of higher importance than the audio. In fact, anything you do could be interpreted as the 'command' trigger so be mindful of what you want to set as the command. Smell though, for a dog, is the most important and reliable sense. For 99% of dogs, smell is the most important sense closely followed by observation (physical) and then the physical which often overrides the verbal.

Dogs have a field of view of circa 250 degrees whereas we, as humans, are limited to 180 degrees. You can test this, after you feel the command has been embedded, by standing completely still and looking away from your dog (or turn your back) and then issue a verbal command – does your dog respond? No, then it has taken something else as the trigger. You can always combine body (hand) signals with the verbal as both will reinforce each other if done so consistently and with good timing.

Rule #3:   **Be patient**. It can be a slow process and only via consistent repetition will the command(s) take hold. Even if your dog learns quickly you will still need to practice this often in order for this to become embedded (habituated).

Rule #4:   **Be calm**. It can be frustrating when things take longer than anticipated, or your dog does not seem to respond in the way you want but you need to remain calm and focused. Your dog will 'read' your frustration and focus on those energies instead as (going back to primal level thinking) you are presenting signs of a negative experience and it is wiser for a dog to focus on this rather than anything you are trying to do. Remember the 5 Cs.

Rule #5:   **1st GOLDEN RULE** – **Always present your marker (reward sound) within a second, or fraction of a second, of the desired action**. This does not mean you necessarily issue the treat at the same time but the marker sound must be made (almost) immediately after the action. In fact, it is best not give the reward at the same time as giving the marker sound as this will confuse your dog. The marker is a "well done – something good is coming" statement and you will have a few seconds after this to issue the reward which is the 'something good' that it will be expecting. Adopting the delayed reward approach means that you build in impulse control automatically and you can, with a bit of practice, start linking commands to build a sequence of actions and reward the sequence at the end.

Rule #6.   **Small steps**. Reward each positive step of the journey and you will get to the destination (desired outcome). If your dog is not quite getting it, then look to reward the effort that is almost correct and then build from there. By rewarding the effort and building bit by bit each successful step, no matter how small, your dog will eventually piece it all together and you will get the desired outcome. Small steps equal great strides.

Rule #7:   **2nd GOLDEN RULE** - **When the fun stops stop**. If it is not fun for you then it is highly unlikely that it will be fun for your dog. Dogs can smell chemical changes such as increased cortisol, adrenalin etc, in your body and other minute changes in your body. So if you are getting stressed or frustrated your dog will know it, no matter how good your poker face is.

Rule #8:   **3rd GOLDEN RULE** – **Repeat, repeat, repeat, rest**. Repetition is key to success but so are regular rest periods. This should never be a matter of endurance.

Not bad eh. No rules for your dog but 8 rules for you.

Types of Training

Basically, there are 3 types of training techniques (methods); lure, shaping and observation. For arms-reach training (sit, heel etc) I tend to use the lure. I hold a treat in front of the dog's nose and teach the dog to follow my hand knowing that wherever the head goes the body will do the opposite. For example, to get a dog to sit then I lure the dog's head up and let the its backside (naturally) land on the ground. As soon as this happens, I release the marker sound (confirming to the dog that this is a good response) and give the dog its reward. You will note I have not issued any instruction as yet. I aim to add the instruction when the dog has made several successful repetitions of the required exercise.

When I get to a point where the dog is consistently delivering the response I want, again using sit as an example, I will introduce the 'sit' command as soon as its bum hits the floor then affirm my satisfaction with the marker sound and reward. I will repeat this over and over until I am satisfied that the command converts to the action in the dog's mind. I will eventually the phase out the treats but continue with the marker. Lure training is placing a treat in front of your dog and moving your hand in a way that gets your dog to sit, lie down, roll-over etc. Essentially, you are manipulating a dogs natural movements and stance etc in order to get it to do something specific. Soon you will be able to just issue the command, without luring, get the action and then give the reward.

Shaping behaviour is a bit more complicated and requires very good (reward) timing as fundamentally you are waiting for, or encouraging, a behaviour/action to happen naturally (via manipulating the environment) and 'marking' the 'correct' action when it happens. You can then build, bit by bit, a chain of actions by adding a new action and rewarding at the last action completed. Once you have built the sequence via the continual 'marking' of the last action achieved you can then work-in a command at the final (end) stage. Again, eventually via continual practice, your dog will make the association of the action required to the sound and you will eventually be able to issue the command in advance and your dog should respond accordingly.

Shaping training, mainly a using clicker, is very effective in trick, distance work or competitive (i.e. flyball) training where you need to put together a string of different activities back-to-back often from distance. Shaping can be great as it is the dog that is in control of the learning and only hears the reward marker when it does all, or part, of a desired activity or activities. For example, if I want to train my dog to sit on a plinth I would build up the actions and break the reward markers down like so...

a) Mark when he passes close to the plinth
b) Mark when he looks at the plinth (when in close proximity)
c) Mark when he puts a paw on the plinth
d) Mark when he puts 2 paws on the plinth
e) Mark when he walks over, the plinth
f) Mark when he stands on the plinth
g) Mark when he stands for duration on the plinth
h) Introduce the command 'plinth' when he stands on the plinth followed by the marker
i) Build out the duration (see duration training below)

Dogs also learn via observation. An example of this is when your dog raises its paw when you put your hand out. If you reward this then your dog is likely to repeat it. If you also add in the command "give me a paw" when it does raise its paw then it will, eventually, link the command to the desired action. Once your dog understands this 'link' then you should be able to issue the "give me a paw" command and get the 'paw' action from it in response.

A couple more important things to remember when training a dog. The aim is for the dog to work out what the correct response is and being patient is key to this. In addition, only reward actions or behaviours that you have actually requested as dogs, especially active dogs, will try and work out what gets rewards and perform the action(s) with, or without, your instruction. You should always be the one to initiate instruction and reward only for correct responses thereof.

Take care to ensure that you never reward actions that you have not requested. If you do, your dog will take from this that 'asking' (which is basically demanding/begging) gets results (in terms of getting a reward) and this may become a default habit possibly undermining all of your training efforts. Further to this, some dogs look for short-cuts and try to cut to the chase going straight to the last action which they think will trigger the reward. This should never be rewarded else your dog will be less inclined in future to conduct the behaviour(s) in full. Remember, no exceptions as dogs don't do exceptions.

A quick word on 'active' and 'reactive' dog types. Active dogs generally work out that they are in control of the behaviour(s) that delivers the goodies. They will often go through their full repertoire of 'tricks' unrequested in order to try and entice a reward or when they are not sure what it is that is required. Reactive dogs tend to deliver the response if they can work it out, try to give a response but give up fairly quickly if this does not get rewarded or give nothing at all if they are unclear or confused. Active dogs are generally easier to train as they are more generally more intelligent, more curious and more motivated by the reward and thus will do anything they can to get it.

Using either lure, shaping or observation training techniques we need to ensure that we set the right training conditions. As noted previously, for best results, initial training should be done in a distraction free environment. You can add distractions in once the training has been well rehearsed and adopted (fault free) by your dog. In fact, solid training should be able to be performed under the 3 environmental conditions of distraction, duration and distance.

Once you have got the required response in distractive conditions you can add duration. You may have to revert to a distraction free environment initially for optimum results. Duration training is where you get the desired response from a command but you don't want to release your dog from it immediately. For example, you issue a command sit and you want your dog to sit there for 30 seconds or so. To achieve this you need to set 'stay' and 'release' commands. Again, this could be anything you want it to be but has to be different from the original command and your 'okay' marker. I use "wait" as my holding command and 'release' as my leave command. What happens now is I issue the original command, get the desired response but instead of issuing the marker noise (i.e. okay) I sound my 'wait' command and wait a few seconds then issue a release command (i.e. release, come etc) and encourage my dog to leave the spot to come to me and reward it accordingly. I gradually extend the time between the wait and release commands. I also use my body shape to help embed the command by putting my hand face up to my dog (as if to signal stop) whilst issuing the wait command. Thereafter, when releasing my dog, I use my hands to beckon my dog over to me.

The next condition is distance. Basically, you should be able to issue the command irrespective of proximity between you and your dog and for your dog to perform the action required, assuming it can see and/or hear you of course. To achieve this, you will again need to start within a distraction free environment. Once your dog has got the command reaction down pat then take a step or two away from your dog then issue the instruction. If your dog performs as required then increase the distance by another one or two steps. Repeat this until you can stand quite some distance away, issue the command and your dog adheres to it.

With the above conditions only ever introduce distractions once your dog reliably performs the required actions distraction-free. Training is all about building blocks and timing. You should always be working at your dog's pace and never try to short-cut the training as this will lead to inconsistent results and no long-term benefit.

The timing of the command to response to marker is crucial. The actual delivery of the reward need not be immediate and need not be every time. In fact, you will get better results if the reward is delayed and random. It is hard not to issue the (okay) marker and (reward) treat at the same time but with practice you will get it and, believe me, your dog will get it too. That being said, the dog should always understand that the reward is in direct response to the behaviour borne from the command.

It is also important to re-state that pessimistic dogs will train at a slower pace and will look for guidance more often. That being said, once they have got it then they have really got it and it takes longer for that trained response to be lost or forgotten.

Note: You will want to reduce, if not, phase out treats when the training objectives have been achieved and regularly performed. However, when phasing out treats don't do this in linear form or regular pattern as your dog will work it out and then only respond effectively when it is 'guaranteed' to get a treat. Some dogs may tend to take treats for granted if they are rewarded 100% of the time therefore the 'need to impress' will lessen as will the promptness and effectiveness of the required behavioural reaction. If a dog does not know on what occasion they will get the reward it will maintain the behaviour (and behaviour standards) in the hope that 'this is the time' that it will get the reward. This is called the gambler's paradox (or the 'near miss effect') and it works in both humans and dogs. A gambler will never lose when using a slot machine as they, in their mind, will always 'nearly win' therefore will be self-motivated to continue trying. Dogs work on the same principle with training (not slot machines thankfully) as they will think 'this' is the time I will get the reward, but you do have to still reward them every now and again to maintain this incentive.

Remember, as stated in the previously noted 8 rules (2nd golden rule) keep training sessions short but frequent. If your dog starts to show lack of response, or interest, then take a break. There is little point progressing when only one of you is interested. Conversely if you end training (always on a high and with lots of praise) then you will leave your dog wanting more which will make it a whole lot easier to pick up where you left off going forward.

Setting the goals

Unfortunately, I often see training and trainers go through the motions and conduct training-by-numbers using pre-set generic methodologies. That's not really my style as I am what could possibly be called an objectives trainer and I would urge you to become the same. This is probably borne from the fact that I am a behaviourist first and trainer second and, in that regard, setting achievable and bespoke objectives is fundamental to my successes. What I mean by this is that standard training usually means that if a dog does not get something right then it is doing something wrong. For me, the dog does not do anything wrong, ever! The dog is doing what it thinks is correct but may not fully understand what's required or, on occasion, just be a bit too playful or unfocused. They may also be in their rebellious period (from 5 months to 9 months) and develop a bit of a stubborn streak and push the boundaries a bit more than we would generally appreciate. Or it could be a Beagle!

For me, if something goes wrong and you are not getting the desired outcomes then the message and motivation is not connecting with your dog and you need to address this. Dogs love learning so you should love teaching. The old adage of "if they don't learn the way you teach then teach the way they learn" is as true for dogs as it is for people. I promote flexibility and fun and, if you take anything away at all from reading this book, I would like it to be that.

The above being said, I am not saying that there is not a place for group training nor training-by-numbers as these can be very important and, in general, they do play vital community roles. These can also provide decent information in techniques to show how to give our dogs some basic obedience and discipline. I am also not saying that if someone is a dog behaviourist then they will make a good trainer or if they are not then they will be a bad trainer as nothing would be further from the truth. Dog training and dog behaviour are two completely different sides of the same coin. A dog trainer will understand what to do to get a dog to respond in a certain way whereas a behaviourist will understand why the dog has responded in the way it has. I know some excellent trainers who get fantastic results without in-depth understanding of the cognitive mechanics of a dog and some behaviourists who would struggle conducting a basic obedience class. The key is all in the results so ask around, check reviews and do some homework to find out who seems to be highly regarded in your community.

Trainer or behaviourist aside it is important that your dog learns the following 8 basic training requirements. Numbers 7 and 8 are rarely taught in group training classes but, for me, are a vital requirement for all dogs, therefore you may need to seek 1-1 support for these if you feel the guides I have set out below do not suffice.

The 8 basic training requirements are: -

1) **Sit** – This is the first thing any dog should know and getting this in the bag helps greatly with other training and, believe it or not, resolving some behavioural issues.

2) **Sit/Stay** – Or just stay to be honest because if a dog is sitting it is not going anywhere anyway. The variation on this is down/stay (see point 3).

3) **Lie down** – Yep, the good old lie down (down stay) which is good for general obedience.

4) **Walk on lead** – Again, another fundamental which provides knock-on benefits elsewhere in the development cycle.

5) **Recall** – Absolutely crucial if you ever want to walk your dog off-lead.

6) **Look at me** – Eye contact is key to control. You, as the resource provider, should be the centre of your dog's world and they should look to you for guidance (quite literally)

7) **Meet and greet** – Or just good social (introduction) manners.

8) **Emergency stop** – This allows you to get your dog to 'stop and drop' from distance giving you the reassurance that it

will not run across roads, go up to other dog/people etc and always stay under your control.

I will now go into more detail on how to train the 8 core training requirements. It is important to note however, that you should not ask for a behaviour (issuing instruction) before you have taught it. That may sound like common-sense but you will be amazed how many people issue an instruction such as "sit" and just keep repeating the instruction with the hope that the dog will eventually understand what is being said and what is to be done. In actuality what often happens is that these people keep making these sounds, the dog gets confused, tired or wishes to appease and sits then they make a fuss of them (and possibly give them a treat) and the dog works out what happened and retains this knowledge. Dogs do, in effect, teach themselves but there are easier and quicker ways of getting there and the guides below, I hope, will help you achieve these.

It is also important to remind you that you are incentivising your dog to give the required behaviour and sometimes you are up against a dog that is possibly dealing with other temptations. Given this, you need to ensure that you give your dog every reason to pay attention to you. You should look at the rewards (treats, toys, praise) you intend to give your dog as 'currency' and accept that sometimes you need to pay £1 but other times £5. It's all down to what other currencies you are up against.

So here we go: -

1. Sit (lure training)

Take a treat and move it toward and over your dog's nose.
Your dog should naturally follow the treat moving its head
up toward the treat and thus its bum will naturally go down
onto the floor. It may take a few attempts but once the dog
gets it will not take long to for this to become a natural
action. Once this happens on a regular basis you can
introduce the word 'sit' and this, via repeated association,
will become a predictor (command request) and you will be
able to verbally issue this command and your dog should
comply.

2. Sit/Stay (lure & observational training)

Once your dog it able to sit on command you can introduce
distance and expect your dog to stay in position and not
move away. To do this you issue the sit command and,
assuming compliance, raise your hand (in the stop position)
and take a step or two away and then immediately go back to
your original position directly in front of the dog and reward
it. It is important that the dog gets the reward, and the
"good" marker (sound) when you return and not when you
are at distance. This will ensure that your dog will learn to
wait for the reward and not try and short cut it.

Repeat the above increasing the distance by one or two steps each time. If your dog looks to get up take a brisk step forward and reassert your hand in the stop position and say "stay". If your hand was already up in the stop position when your dog looks to move the take it back quickly and then immediately restate it in the stop position and say "stay". Repeat the above until you can get 10 or so steps away, return and issue the reward. At this point you should introduce duration to the stay and to do this you do not immediately return but wait a second or so before returning then you issue the treat reward.

From this point it is all about repeating the exercise increasing the distance and/or duration. If you get to a point where you dog just will not stay in position then go back to the last point where you had full compliance and rebuild.

3. **Lie Down** (lure training)

As with the sit procedure this time lure the treat down towards the ground and slightly away from your dog so that it needs to stretch to get it and, hopefully, by doing so it will lie down. Once the dog lies down then reward it with the treat being as close to the ground as possible. Again, if your dog is not getting this straight way just repeat and give plenty of praise and treats when it does.

4. Loose Lead Walking (lure, shaping & observational training)

Dogs tend to pull on a lead because walking at human pace is an unnatural activity for them. On top of this the world is an exciting/intriguing place so why would they not want to get there quickly, even if they don't know where 'there' is. For most dogs, the world is an exciting place that is to be fully explored, often at pace. However, as responsible guardians and for their safety and protection, you need to be in control of the walk. Don't let your dog walk you!

Before you look at the different methods you can use to achieve a better response whilst out on a walk you will firstly need to understand the reason for the walk. This may sound obvious but it isn't. It is important that you understand the purpose of the walk, in order to enable you to set the appropriate expectation of what you want from your dog during the walk.

For me, the three main walk functions are '*business*' (going to the toilet, basic exercise (i.e. street walks around the block), getting some fresh air), '*play*' (playing games, longer duration walks, scent walks, general activity walks, pack walks etc) and '*training*' walks. These are not mutually exclusive but if you do have a core (walk) objective then you can manage the walking experience and perceived outcomes much better.

The reason I have noted the different walk types is that in the 'training' walk you will be doing things that you would not normally do but will be doing so in order to create control and guidance techniques that your dog will benefit from on non-training walks. There is no destination or other objective in a training walk other than to help your dog learn by it working out what makes progress and what does not.

However, before you set out on any walk (training or otherwise) you need to ensure that your dog is in the right state of mind allowing you, and your dog, to set off with the right energy and focus. If your dog is energised and unfocused it will be like a coiled spring before you even leave the house. This will make things very difficult for you to get your dog's focus (on you) when out on the walk as, without this focus, then you will have little, or no, control and influence over your dog. The best 'loose lead' walking training starts before you have left the house and even before you have put the lead on your dog. To help with this the following is a pre-walk (or pre-conditioning) program.

Step 1: Get up and pick up your dog's lead (or go through any action you would normally do before you initiate a walk). If your dog goes into a high arousal mode and barks/jumps/spins etc then place the item(s) back (or reverse what you were doing) and do something else instead. There is no requirement to issue any instruction as your dog needs to work out what is happening for itself.

Step 2: Repeat step 1 until you get to the stage of connecting the lead to your dog. If he/she returns to displaying a high energy outburst then calmly remove the lead, put it away and turn your attention elsewhere. Again, there is no need to verbally interact with your dog. As in step 1 only progress when your dog is in a calm state.

Step 3: Once you have managed to pick up the lead and put it on your dog whilst keeping him/her within the calm zone then you can head towards the door. However, should your dog's energies rise again then close the door (if opened), unclip the lead and put everything away and turn your focus elsewhere. You are letting your dog know that you are in charge of the walk and it will only commence once he/she is in a calm state. It may take some time initially but, after a few repetitions, your dog will get it.

Step 4: False Starts: To ensure that your dog understands that picking up the lead and collar does not always mean going for a walk, randomly pick up the lead and go and do something else (i.e. make a cup of tea) whilst still holding the lead in your hand. Then place it back to where you normally would (still not giving your dog any interaction) and go do something else. This will, eventually teach your dog to disassociate the picking up of the lead/collar with always going for a walk. This is important as dogs always try to pre-empt and short-cut matters in order to 'speed up' the process and, in their mind, achieve the outcome far sooner.

Step 5: Do likewise with each action in connection with the pre-walk routine and onto leaving the house maintaining the same principles as noted above. This will set out the framework to your dog that calmness gets rewards (and progress) and manic high energy does not.

The above should help you get your dog into the right energy mode and be more focused on you.

Now onto to the loose lead program. There are several ways to combat lead pulling. Here are TEN of them.

None of the methods below use 'lead correction' techniques (sharply pulling back on the lead) which, personally, I don't recommend or like. I also think this doesn't work long term and is likely to break the trust your dog has in you as a guardian and protector.

1. **Stop Start Method**: If your dog pulls the lead tight then just stop. No touch, no talk and no eye contact. Once the lead slackens (it may take a while so be patient – it will be worth it) then proceed (no talk or instruction). He/she

will probably turn to look at you as if to say "what's going on". If this happens then praise this with a "great" or "good boy/girl" and start moving again. The basic rule here is that if the lead tightens then movement stops and when the lead slackens then movement recommences.

2. **The No Direction Method**: If your dog wants to get there in a hurry then by sharply changing direction every 5-7 steps this will confuse it as to where you are going. Eventually your dog will look to you to 'hand over' direction control as it will not be able to work it out for itself. Once you get to this point you can decrease the regularity of the direction changing until you get to a point where you think your dog has 'got it' and you don't need to perform this action anymore. If your dog does resume the pulling the you can always resurrect this training method.

3. **The Staggered Progress Method**: Walk backwards and forwards. Go forward 5 steps and back 3, forward 6 and back 7, random steps forward and back etc. As with the 'no direction method' you retain the walk control as your dog will not be able to apply a linear strategy to the walk. If a dog cannot predict the destination then it will look to you for guidance. As above you can reduce, or eliminate this, as your dog learns to rely and take direction guidance from you.

4. **The Check Back Method**: In this method slow down your walking pace until your dog looks around at you as if to say "hurry up". At this point, give him/her some praise and/or a treat then move on by picking up the pace again. Repeat this until your dog get to the point that it turns its head around and looks up at the first sign of slowing down. At this point issue a command such as "walk nice" then move on at a pace comfortable to you. Repeat this ongoing. Soon you should be able to issue the command "walk nice" and your dog will make the association of this sound with the pace experienced previously and move into this stride.

5. **The Hand Feed Treat Method**: Get some treats and place them within your hand and make a fist. Let your dog smell the clenched fist with the treat inside and the step off keeping you hand in view of your dog. Randomly slightly loosen your fist and let your dog nibble at the treat, whilst you continue to walk, and then tighten up your hand again. Repeat this ongoing until your dog is regularly checking back to see if it can get a bit of a treat which should, naturally, loosen the lead as it will no longer be pulling forward but instead looking for the opportunity to get a treat. You can reduce the treat rewards you give as your dog becomes more compliant but never look to reduce the praise.

6. **The Dropped Treat Method**: As with the 'hand feed treat method' you do similar but this time, instead of your dog nibbling at the treats in your hand, you drop a treat to the side of you (the same side of your dog), or at your feet, regularly and randomly for your dog to get from the ground. Take care to drop the treat near you and not in front of you so your dog will have no reason to pull on the lead to get the treat.

7. **The Zone Dropped Treat Method**: As with the 'dropped treat method' you do similar but this time you aim to 'throw' the treat slightly to the side of you or _slightly_ behind you in order that your dog has to stop pulling in order to get the reward. For this to work effectively, assuming your dog is pulling forward, you will need to get your dog's attention before you throw the treat down. You can get your dog's attention by making any sound (or command) in a higher-than-normal (excited attention grabbing) tone and then throw the treat. The aim is to ensure that your dog sees where you have thrown the treat. Repetition of this should lead your dog to regularly (visually) check-in with you to see if you are going to throw a treat.

8. **The 'Look at Me' Method**: This ensures that your dog's focus is on you. If you do not have your dog's focus on

you it will be on everything else but and you will be relegated to the level of 'little' or 'no' interest and it may turn into your dog walking you rather than you walking your dog. I have detailed how to achieve 'look at me' in point 6 (below). To bed this in when out on a walk I recommend using the 'look at me' command every 4 or 5 steps initially and, assuming your dog is responding correctly and consistently, then slowly increase the amount of steps between each command. You will eventually get to a point where you will only need to issue the 'look at me' command every now and again or when you want your dog to focus on you rather than something else that may be on the horizon.

It is important to note though that the 'look at me' command works best when your dog is calm and in a 'thinking' state. If your dog is amped up, over aroused or highly emotional then this command is unlikely to work and you will need to get your dog out of the emotional state and back into a thinking state (see section on dog reactivity).

9. **The 'Squeaky Toy' Method**: The aim of this technique is to immediately direct your dog's attention toward you and, of course, reward it for doing to. A good way to grab a dog's attention is to introduce a sound that cuts through whatever it has chosen to focus on and redirect

its focus to whatever has generated the sound. From experience I have found that a squeaky toy seems to have universal doggy appeal and it is great from getting your dog's attention when out on a walk. Be mindful though that the sound of a squeaky toy can carry for quite a remarkable distance, especially given the superior hearing capabilities of dogs, therefore this technique is not recommended if other dogs are nearby.

So, to get this to work whilst on a walk then as soon as you feel your dog is going to start pulling then 'squeak' the toy. Note, I have said when you feel that your dog is going to start pulling and not when it is actually pulling. We don't want to inadvertently reward the act of the 'pull' therefore keen observation and timing are crucial here.

Once your dog has turned to investigate where the noise is coming from give it plenty of praise and/or a treat then change direction and continue the walk. Repeat this throughout ensuring that you maintain your dog's interest in the 'squeak' by rewarding it each time it turns to you to investigate. Changing direction is also an important component here as we are looking to totally break away from what had previously raised our dog's interest.

Continue to repeat this exercise until such times as your dog is pre-empting the squeak (and reward) whereby you can now start to reward the actual 'looking to you' (checking-back) from your dog who has anticipated you squeaking the toy rather than from the actual sound of the squeak itself. From herein you can start to reduce the treats and the changing of direction and build this into a more natural 'walk'. If at anytime your dog goes back to the old routine then just pare back to the point where it last worked and rebuild.

10. **The 'backwards forwards' Method**: The primary principle for this method is to maintain encouragement and engagement between you and your dog.

To start turn and face your dog then take a few steps back enticing your dog to follow. Once your dog follows go another dew steps then turn and walk forward. Walk forward for another few steps then turn and face your dog again. If possible, without stopping walk a few steps backwards again enticing your dog to follow. Once your dog catches up with you again then turn around and walk forward.

Keep the walking backward then forward going but, if your dog is engaging with you and not trying to pull ahead, then extend the time between backward and forward walking.

Once you get to a point where your dog is engaged in this game then start to make the 'walking forward' portion of this activity longer than the walking backward element. The objective is to reduce the walking backward portion to rare and occasional rather than the frequency you had started out with. The rest is rinse and repeat ensuring that you keep extending the walking forward element of this game.

Note: For effective loose lead walking, no matter the technique you choose to employ it is important that you always try to remain as loose and tense-free as possible. If not, you could be telegraphing to your dog your anxiety and, in turn, be telling your dog that they also need to be tense too. The key is always to reward a loose lead but, as stated previously, never jerk back the lead (lead correction) when your dog pulls as this will be uncomfortable for your dog, possibly hurt it, may increase its tenseness and possibly reduce the trust your dog has with you. Positive reinforcement is, for me, always a better option.

5. Recall (shaping and observational training)
The key to getting your dog back when you call its name is to be more appealing or interesting to it than what surrounds it

or what it is focused on. This is often easier said than done but certainly not impossible irrespective of breed. I have all too often heard the line "he/she won't come back because he/she has a high prey drive" or variations on that theme. Yes, this is a factor, and very much a significant factor, but it is certainly not a barrier.

In respect of breed, and prey drive, as long as you satisfy your dog's propensities via regular games, within controlled environments of course, then their hunger to exercise these elsewhere will be lessened; not wholly eradicated, but very much reduced.

A quick word of advice before I detail some recall training techniques. If your dog runs off or just won't come back then, if it is safe to do so, then try turning your back on it and walking away whilst still calling it over. Creating distance from your dog should either trigger its' desire to get back to you or, at the very least, its curiosity in looking to find out what you find more interesting that what it is focused on. Dogs always want what is not theirs and crave the things they don't have, or, very often, just want to find out what is more interesting than what they have found to do and, because of this, they should come over to you to investigate.

Even if you don't have the confidence or you don't think it is appropriate given where you and your dog are please note that unless you really have to then never go toward your dog shouting for it to come back. By doing this you are providing no reason for your dog to return to you because you are going to your dog!

Also, should you feel you need to, running after your dog is a pointless and counter-productive exercise as you will, in all likelihood, not be able to catch it and, in your dog's mind, you will have started a fun game of chase.

With recall training it is always best to initiate training in a distraction free securely enclosed environment if at all possible. If the environment cannot be enclosed, then you will need to use a long (5m, 7m or 10m) training lead to ensure that you can always regain control of your dog if required.

The principle of recall is quite simple. The requirement is that you call your dog by its name and it returns to you. The problem is that there are other things around it that may be more interesting, fun and exciting than you. The other problem is that, when your dog refuses to come back, we often get annoyed, concerned and exasperated raising our voice and stress levels. This will not go unnoticed by your dog and will give it even less reason to return to you. Think about it would you go back to someone who is screaming like a banshee and that you know is going to get on your case when you go over? No, neither will your dog. Your dog will know, from past experience, that it is going to pay a price when it eventually returns to you so why not make it worthwhile in the meantime and stay away and play a bit longer? I mean if you are going to do the time anyway then why not do the crime?

To combat this, you need to create a desire for your dog to come to you over and above any temptation that there may be elsewhere. In order to achieve this outcome you need to be the biggest attraction around. Seriously, you are often competing with temptations that can, to your dog, be way more satisfying and rewarding that what it thinks you will provide. However, you can overcome this and create a strong desire in your dog to return to you by being either:

1. Being super exciting/interesting
2. Being super rewarding
3. Being both of the above

Given the importance and the potential consequences of this when it fails then this is one training program that I would recommend that you train, test, review comprehensively daily for many years, if not life. Even if you feel that your dog has 'got this in the bag' I would still look to test this daily, and in all circumstances and environments, to ensure that when you actually need to use it then you can 99% rely on it. No dog will ever give you 100% guaranteed reliability because sometime life provides temptations, or situations, that your dog can either not resist or is compelled to get away from fast. Anybody that tells you that you can get 100% of anything in a dog, actually in people too, is not living in the real world. It's not if, but when, the '1% exception' will arise but the crucial thing to take away from this 1% situation is when it does arise is what did you learn, what can be changed to protect from it happening again and how can you, and your dog, rebuild? Don't get mad, get smart!

The first part of the recall training program is to decide what the reward is going to be. Given the importance of this exercise, I would suggest using a specific and unique high-value reward for this training program that you know really resonates with your dog and it will do almost anything for. If this needs to be a piece of chicken, turkey, favourite toy etc then so be it. The key here is that your dog only gets this reward in this exercise and at no other time. This is a one-time deal and if your dog wants this badly enough then it should 'seize the opportunity' when it is presented. Once you have decided on the reward then it is time to pair the reward with the (recall) command.

Within a controlled environment with absolutely no distractions give your dog your return command (i.e. "Piper come here!") in a low and boring tone then immediately reward your dog. Repeat this a few times then rest. After a short break resume this exercise but raise your tone slightly. Again, repeat and rest. Now take a decent break before you continue.

Once you resume again pick up at the last tone level and repeat. Once your dog is responding well to this then up the tone again. The principle here is that you want to continue the exercise until you get to the level you would get to if you were to shout your dog back. Remember to keep taking breaks and don't try to rush this by trying to 'bag it' in one day or a few days etc. It is far too important to be rushed.

Once you get to the point where you are rewarding at the vocal level you would be using when calling your dog back then you can go to the next stage. At this stage when you issue the command (at the top vocal level) then immediately take a few steps back from your dog. This will result in your dog having travel farther back to you in order to get to you and the reward. Always give the reward when your dog is next to you and preferably sitting down. Repeat this exercise moving back a bit more each time.

The next stage is to issue the command, turn your body away from your dog, walk away a few steps and wait for your dog to come around to the front of you. When this happens definitely get your dog to sit before issuing the reward.

Repeat this exercise increasing the distance and always reward your dog when it returns and sits in front of you.

If you get to a point where your dog is not responding as you would like then pare back to the distance, position or tone your dog was happy to respond to and rebuild from there. Again, you are not looking to rush things but instead to embed and reward the command to the action. Remember, this is the only exercise where your dog will get this particular reward therefore, if your dog values it enough (and it should), it will not want to miss this opportunity to get it.

Once you have got to the stage where you can issue the command, walk away and your dog reliably returns and sits in expectation of getting this reward you can add in a 'lock' by increasing your excitement appeal. You do this by increasing your tone to high pitch and jumping and dancing around like someone possessed. Yes really. Dr Ian Dunbar calls this the 'jolly routine' and it really does appeal to dogs. Your dog will not only be engaged by the tone of your voice but also the animation of your body and will want to come over to investigate what all of the fuss is about. Once it comes over, get it to sit and reward it then follow on with some high-excitement praise and play. This will 'lock' in the desire to come to you when you call as the reward it gets (treat, praise and some play) is so super amazing (high value and rarely given). Wow, what's not to like!

Now, if jumping about squealing with excitement is not your thing, and to be honest it is not mine, then the training program detailed up to that point will work but the latter exercise is a fantastic behavioural response lock.

Once you have achieved the above in a controlled environment then the next step is to try this in an uncontrolled environment. Remember though, build it up in a quieter area and, again, start at close quarters then build up the distance. I would definitely recommend the use of a long training lead (5m+) initially when working in open and uncontrolled environments.

After a few weeks of reliable correct responses from your dog you can build what I call a *super recall*. The super recall training is basically the same training program but replacing your voice with a whistle. The sound of a whistle is more defined than your voice and will carry over longer distances.

Another good trick is to ensure that when you call your dog back and go through the process of putting on its lead that this does not always mark the end of the fun time. If your dog associates you wishing to put the lead back on as the signal for the end of play time then your dog is not going to be motivated to return to you. Therefore, regularly call your dog back, put its lead on, reward it and enjoy some play time then unclip its lead again and let it go play elsewhere. This will ensure that your dog will never be able to work out if the lead going on means more fun or time to go home.

6. **Look at me** (lure, shaping & observational training)

This is a great game/training program as you can (eventually) use this "instruction" in lots of ways and many different circumstances. This is especially important if you need to divert your dog's attention from something that it may adversely react to. This game is not only a great bonding tool, therefore its importance in relationship and control cannot be under-estimated, but also the foundation for productive training and development.

To achieve this, get a treat and hold it in front of your nose. As soon as your dog looks at it (and by default you) then give it the treat. There is no verbal instruction at this point. Repeat several times until you feel that you dog understands it gets the treat by looking at the treat (and, of course, the you). Once your dog is doing this consistently then introduce a "look at me" command just before you give out the treat. Note: don't give the treat straight away after issuing the instruction – if you wait a couple of seconds before you give your dog the treat then this will embed the command.

Now repeat this exercise but this time hold the treat to the side of your face. This time reward your dog when it looks at you and not the treat (even if it is a quick glance as small wins are better than no wins). Again, issue the instruction "look at me" before you give your dog its reward. Repeat this with the aim of moving your hand away from your face (eventually through to full extension) and reward your dog when it looks at you and not the treat upon hearing the command "look at me".

Once your dog does this consistently, test it frequently and randomly to ensure the when your dog hears "look at me" that it understands, without doubt, that he/she is to look at you. You can phase out the treats throughout time once your dog gets it but always retain the praise.

7. **Meet and greet** (lure, shaping and observational Training)

If your dog is not at all comfortable with other dogs then it is counter-productive to force 'socialisation' on it and, by doing so, it may lead to a more fearful and reactive dog. Conversely you may have a dog that just wants to play and interact with every other dog it sees. Whatever type of dog you have it is important that it knows how to introduce itself to other dogs in a socially acceptable and controlled way.

To successfully achieve this you must ensure that you understand and respect your dog and the signals that your dog may be giving you. If your dog is naturally fearful of other dogs then you need to take great care and progress things at a much slower pace and keep your dog under threshold at all times.

If your dog is the opposite and tends to barge into play then you need to let it know that all good things are controlled by you. Only when your dog behaves in an acceptable manner will it get the reward of meeting the other dog, or dogs. There is absolutely no defence for any dog that goes bounding over to any other dog (or person) unrestrained. This is irrespective of what the dog's intentions are – it is an uncontrolled and potentially out-of-control dog.

Added to this you do not know how the other dog, or other dog guardian, is going to view this or how they will react. It is not uncommon for the dog being rapidly approached to take exception to it and look to deal with it head on and sometimes the outcome is disastrous. To be honest, this is a possible outcome from the other dog's guardian too. Good manners, in both people and dogs, are appreciated and dogs tend to show their disapproval without hesitation if they feel that is what is required.

For training acceptable 'meet and greets' I have two main approaches; one for fear reactive dogs and one of overly-playful dogs.

a. Fear reactive dog

I cover this in more detail in the chapter 'common issues and behavioural challenges'. The key here is not to put your dog in a situation that you know it will feel uncomfortable by forcing your dog to meet other dogs when it would clearly prefer not to. Please respect its desire to stay away and look to slowly build its acceptance of other dogs being around via having play, training and other 'fun' experiences in the vicinity, but not right next to, the other dogs. If at any time your dog is telling you that it is not comfortable and wishes to move away then please listen to it and move away. You are looking to eventually reverse your dog's negative perception of being around other dogs (counter conditioning) by allowing it to learn that there is nothing to fear and, moreover, it can be (eventually) a fun and rewarding experience.

If your dog is reactive and you are concerned that other dogs may come over to it to interact then you can invest in Hi-Viz dog jacket or collar and lead, that has written on it, in big and bold text (on a yellow background), 'nervous', 'nervous dog', or 'I need space'. This will alert other responsible owners to your situation and, hopefully, they will guide their dog away from yours keeping your dog as stress free as possible. I had initially purchased one for my youngest dog, Piper, who was attacked by another dog when a pup whilst in the middle of her fear stage and used it whilst training her to be more accepting of other dogs. I found that most guardians saw this easily, respected it and allowed Piper dog-free space.

For the, thankfully low number of, guardians who do not respect the 'Hi Viz' jacket and message then calmly guide yourself and your dog away from them with no fuss. Don't try and engage with the other guardian, as they are patently too stupid, or inconsiderate, not to heed the message on the (highly visible) jacket, therefore you will just be wasting your time. If needed, you can also body block the other dog's access to your dog and guide away.

b. Playful overly energetic dog

The first thing to note here is that a playful dog that has no manners is just a liable to be attacked as is a dog that is not-so-friendly to other dogs. This may seem a bit odd as it may be the case that we know our dog just wants to play with all of the other dogs it sees, and it may even be super obvious by its vocal and body language that this is the case. However, we are assuming that both the other dog and its guardian are capable of reading this intent and, from my experience, that is not always the case. It may not surprise you that some people are not able to read dog body language. However, it may surprise you to learn that not all dogs are able to read the body and vocal language of other dogs. If this is the case then, often by default, they may go into 'potential threat' mode and react accordingly.

It does not matter what size of dog you have, big or small, if it is bounding over to another dog full on at the rate of knots, then it should come as no surprise that the 'receiving' dog may take exception to this and look to put the offending dog in its place. Think about how you would react if someone came shooting over to you and got right in amongst your face without so much as a how do you do? Exactly. We really cannot expect our dogs to be any different. Good manners are as important to dogs as they are to people.

The key to ensuring that your dog displays acceptable social manners is to, quite simply, teach it. There are four core components to acceptable doggy meet and greet etiquette. These are 'energy', 'approach', 'introduction' and 'engagement or send off'. I have detailed each element and how to effectively teach these to your dog below.

a. Energy
You will note that energy seems to be a constant theme in this book and this reflect how important it really is. When meeting and greeting another dog your dog's energy should always be balanced and calm. Therefore, if your dog raises its energies when moving towards another dog then turn away from the

other dog and create distance taking care not to verbally engage with your dog. The aim here is to teach your dog that it if gets too excited then it will not be rewarded by meeting the other dog but, rather, distance will be created between them. If it is impossible to create distance between the dogs then briskly walk past the other dog taking care not to engage with it or your dog.

It is also a good opportunity to use the 'look at me' exercise when moving to, past, or away from the other dog.

Note, the other dog, or other dogs, energy levels are important also and if they too are too high then, to ensure no adverse reactions, avoid, or abort, the meet and greet. You may well be able to control your dog but you will have little, or no, control over someone else's dog.

Progress only when the penny drops and your dog's energies do not raise 'excitedly'. If your dog is calm then you can allow your dog to get closer and closer to the other dog always ensuring that neither dog's energies go to level 10 (or even 8 or 9). This will take a bit of time as your dog will need to work out for itself what is happening and act accordingly but, if you are consistent and determined, your dog will get it.

b. Approach

It is always best to approach any new dog, irrespective of how your dog reacts, from the rear end, or side (parallel walking), of the other dog rather than face on. If you are able to be downwind of the other dog then all the better. This will enable your dog to pick up a lot of information about the other dog via scent and sight thus reducing its natural curiosity somewhat before the meet.

c. Introduction

Good dog introductions are brief affairs. Basically, it is sniff and move on. I call this the 2-3 second hello. In the initial stages the introduction should be no more than this. As you leave give your dog plenty of praise (and treats possibly) continuing the positive experience whilst moving away from the other dog. What you are teaching your dog here is that there is no need to get overly excited as the satisfaction of the meet is a non, or calm, event and nothing to get too excited about.

d. Engagement

This is the most crucial step as it this will solidify the outcome experience in your dog. You want this to be positive but mostly you want this to be controlled. Initially you, and your dog, should quickly move on after the initial 'meet and greet' of any dog until such times as you are sure that your dog's energies will not rise in an undesired fashion. Your dog will still get the satisfaction of the sight and scent whilst you will get the satisfaction of 'no undesired drama'.

Once you get to the stage where your dog remains calm and you, the other dog and, of course, the other dog's guardian, are quite happy for the dogs to interact (full engagement) then you can stay a bit longer and let the dogs explore each other. However, it is still crucial that you retain control of your dog and don't overstay your welcome. I would recommend a minute or two for the first few engagements then extend thereafter, but only if your dog, and the other dog's energies stay within acceptable levels and there are no signs of potential conflict (growling, staring, bared teeth etc).

8. **Emergency stop and drop** (Observational & Shaping Training)

As with recall this is another important training element that is rarely taught in foundation puppy classes yet can save your dog getting into trouble or even save its life.

There may be times where recall may not be feasible, i.e. if there is a dog/person etc between you and your dog that you do not wish you dog to pass. Therefore, you need a command where you can be assured your dog will stop immediately what it is doing, focus on you and, preferably, lie down in-situ waiting for you to come over to it.

As with recall it is always best to initially train in a secure and distraction free environment then test this frequently in the real world.

Firstly, you need a command. I use "halt" but it can be anything that suits you but its best it is not its name (unless as a suffix) and preferably monosyllabic if possible. Monosyllabic sounds cut through other noise that may be surrounding your dog and acts as an 'action interrupter' grabbing your dog's immediate attention which, in this case, is vital.

You now need a reward. You can use the same high value treat as the recall as, for me, 'recall' and 'halt' are both equal in safety value and compliance for both should be as rock solid as possible.

In the same way you had built the association of the command to the reward with recall you will use the same principle for this exercise. They key difference here is that you want your dog to immediately stop where it is and not to move from where it is when you issue the command. This is why it is important to apply the high-value reward where your dog stopped and not where you are when you issued the command.

To start this training then walk and get your dog to walk by your side (see loose lead walking techniques in this book). You may need to do this via a fixed lead initially if your dog is not great at walking with you off-lead. Assuming your dog is walking close by you then turn towards your dog and issue your 'halt' command in a short and sharp way. Now wait for your dog to stop walking (and hopefully look at you). If your dog does stop, take a step away and raise your hand (with the stop signal) reissue your 'halt' command (not too loud but in an assertive manner) and then do nothing but observe how your dog responds. If your dog does not move forward then step back to it and reward your dog. For best results for this exercise then give the treat from the ground up and not top down. You want your dog to expect the reward from below. However, if your dog does look as if it is going to move forward then re-issue the command and make a small movement as if you are going to walk toward it (but don't).

Your dog should now, hopefully, sit or, at the very least, stay where it is. Repeat this until you dog does not make any attempt to move forward. If you can, try and pre-empt your dog's desire to move and re-issue the 'halt' command at the earliest sign your dog shows of wanting to move.

Repeat this until such times as your dog is standing still most, if not all of the time. You should still only be one step away from your dog.

Once your dog is responding correctly to this command, at close quarters, then you can up the ante and instruct your dog to lie down before you step back and issue the reward. Lying down is a good to have response but not a required response. The important factor is your dog staying in position and not moving.

Repeat the above until your dog responds by staying put (or lying down) 99% of the time. This response should be rock solid before moving to the next stage.

Once you are ready for the next stage then you can take a few steps away before issuing the commend (and the hand action) and hopefully your dog will understand, from the previous training, what it is to do and respond accordingly. If it doesn't then just close the distance a bit and rebuild. If your dog does respond by stopping and, ideally, dropping (lying down) then calmly walk over to the dog, issue some praise and then the reward (from the ground up). Repeat this until your dog is performing this correctly and consistently with no major issues.

From herein it is all about building distance and your vocal volume (as you will may need to issue this instruction from distance and in an emergency). Bear in mind that you should still be working within a distraction free environment just now.

Once you are ready to test this in a place with distractions then do so but start again close in and, again, look to build out and increase the distance bit by bit.

Note, the issuing rewards must always be when you return to the dog and from the ground up. It is also recommended to give your dog plenty of praise and let it know how pleased you are. This will increase its desire to repeat the learned (correct) response.

As with any training, if you go too far too soon then just pare it back to the last step where your dog responded as you wanted restart the training exercise and rebuild.

Again, as with recall, this should be practised daily and over many months to become part of everyday life.

I would like to emphasise it is important that, as with most training programs, you should practice initially in distraction-free areas in order to give yourself and your dog the best chance of success. If you try this in an area where there are lots of distractions, or distractions that your dog thinks will reward it more than the treats, your praise or any play that you are offering, then your training efforts are unlikely to work very well at all.

It is also important to remind you that you should eventually phase out the treats, therefore, once you get solid compliance, especially in areas with distractions, then move to a random issue of treats and then, rarely giving treats. The praise should always be there and does not need phased out.

It is also recommended that you are cognisant of the character and temperament of your dog. If you are working with a confident and energetic dog then you need to slow their world down and initially reward inactivity rather than activity. High energy dogs tend to gorge on play and training opportunities and don't know how to stop or slow down. If this is the case then you need to give your dog lot's of 'time outs' where you stop all interaction, physical and verbal, and allow your dog to 'come down' and learn to be happy and comfortable in its own space where a whole lot of nothing is going on. The eventual aim is to manage your dog's energies and focus to the point that it will take heed of your guidance and motivational enticements.

If you have a nervous and pessimistic dog then reduce the task orientated and instruction based activities and, again initially, concentrate on play and mentally stimulating activities but with no end goals other than activity enjoyment. The aim here is to build confidence in your dog and this can be achieved through free play, mental stimulation and, as with high energy dogs, plenty of time outs (relaxation periods). Please note though, that you do not want to inadvertently reinforce your dog's nervousness or fearfulness by trying to pacify it via cuddles and soft words as this will be counter-productive. Instead, support your dog in building confidence and making good choices and only offer vocal and physical pacification as a last resort and in keeping with the principles contained within the 'talk with purpose' guide noted later in this book.

In all types of dogs, be they confident, nervous, optimistic or pessimistic it is important that, during the first few months of training, you don't verbally interact too much as, for a confident dog, it will mean nothing to it, as it already has a whole lot going on, but will add to its energy levels. For the nervous, or pessimistic dog, your vocal interactions may become a crutch whereby your dog will continue to look toward you for help rather than building its confidence in its own decision making and, because of this, it becomes less self-sufficient and more needy.

The absence of 'chatter' does not mean the absence of influence or control. Oftentimes what is not said is more powerful than what is and, for dogs, less verbal interaction often means less distraction and less confusion. I call this ***dynamic silence*** where you are using the verbal gaps to strengthen the verbal interactions that you do choose to make. Dynamic silence is often also a good way to show your disapproval should you need to. By using your dog's default desire to socialise and interact with you then you are using silence as a guide and not inadvertently rewarding your dog for inappropriate responses or behaviour. Remember, dogs naturally show their disapproval by creating distance and you are doing likewise but in verbal form.

Everyone together

Finally, as with any effective dog training, it is important that everyone adopts the process and principles noted in this book whether they be family, friends or visitors. This will give your dog consistency in the messages conveyed, allow your dog to learn that there are no exceptions and that compliance is always the best option to choose as it gets the best chance of any rewards that may be on offer. Inconsistency in training or commands given will only confuse your dog and may 'teach' it that there are exceptions to the rules.

'ENERGY AND STRUCTURED TRAINING' CHAPTER SUMMARY

- **Physical and mental energy**
- **Low and slow**
- **Manage the environment**
- **Impulse control**
- **Energy burn off**
- **Leadership and control**
- **Positive and negative reinforcement**
- **Positive and negative punishment**
- **The 8 rules of a good training structure**
- **Methods of training**
- **Active and reactive dogs**
- **Distraction, duration and distance**
- **Phasing out treats**
- **Setting the goals**
- **8 Basic training requirements**
- **Everyone together**

Chapter 5: It's Playtime

Play is a vital and enriching element for dogs. Not only does play afford your dog a natural energy release but, in many cases, it builds confidence and also strengthens the trust and bond you and your dog will have. Dog to dog play is often a predatory practice and can, to us, look a bit scary and rough sometimes but this is fairly normal.

Play also releases the feel-good, alertness and relaxation chemicals such as adrenalin* (survival and excitement), serotonin (the mood chemical), endorphin (feel good hormone), dopamine (the pleasure centre), as well as, in some cases, oxytocin (the love hormone) to name but a few. The importance of play cannot be understated as it can satisfy a dog's breed instinct as well as its mental and physical needs resulting in a happier, calmer and more optimistic dog. The positive consequence of a dog with plenty of play in its life will be fewer behavioural issues and an easier and more reliable and compliant dog to train. The old adage of "a tired dog is a good dog" is, in principle, true but an oversimplified generalization that needs to be taken with a pinch of salt. It is energy and **focus** that is crucial to successful training.

Note: Adrenalin release is part of the survival system and can, and will be, released in times of stress also.

Mental stimulation is also an essential requirement for producing a well-balanced dog. In fact, it has been cited that just 10 minutes of brain training for a dog is equal to 30 minutes of physical training. Physically most dogs will be able to go on for hours as they are built for stamina and strength.

If you think about it though, in the modern world, many dogs are left at home for hours on end with little to do but to entertain themselves. It can be like a mental jail. Imagine if you were left at home day in day out with nothing to do but pass time. This is not a criticism but moreover a reflection of the demands of the modern world.

The mental stimulation requirement is often overlooked even though, as previously stated, this element is as equally important as physical exercise is, if not more so. The recent introduction and rise of dog parks, dog sitters, dog walkers and doggy day cares are testament to the modern world impact on our dogs.

Dogs are predisposed to be sociable, self-satisfying and (generally) fun-loving. Dogs also have a natural drive and desire to learn and most dogs, in my experience, thrive with positive reinforcement games and training.

In fact, very often a lot of the behavioural issues I am called upon to provide solutions for often result in more playtime for the dog! The key though is 'play with purpose' where you set end goals and objectives for the play (this becomes structured training). This all being said I do have to add that less confident and nervous dogs will need play <u>without</u> set tasks or milestones (initially) just to help them feel better, build their confidence and become more self-reliant in decision making abilities.

Dog socialisation

I would, at this point, like to say a bit about dog socialisation and bust a few dog socialisation myths. Although dogs have been bred, generation after generation, to be sociable and interact with people, unfortunately, modern living has, in respect of dog to dog interaction, set our dogs back a bit because the opportunities to meet and interact with other dogs have significantly lessened as the decades roll by. We no longer tend to intermingle with each other and often compartmentalise our lives and end up creating online communities rather than real-world ones. Mainly because of this, it seems we have, inadvertently, taught our dogs to segregate as a default rather than integrate.

When I was growing up, a fair few moons ago now, it was not uncommon to see dogs out on the street mixing it up naturally with people and dogs alike. You rarely witnessed, or heard of, squabbles or attacks (although they were not totally unheard of) but, even these, were short mainly bluff and bluster affairs where the dogs involved quickly resolved the issue, made up and moved on. Good dog to dog interaction and sociability was a vital survival skill then. There were occasions where there were dog attacks, on people and other dogs, that were serious but they were the exception rather than the rule and often the result of rough handling or downright abuse by a cruel individual or group.

The creation of first world living and technologically led networking has all but rendered natural face-to-face interactions extinct for many people and dogs. People now tend to interact infrequently via planned work and social events which is all very rigid and constructed. We rarely bump into Mrs Jones in the street and have a good old chinwag putting to right all of the world's ills. We live in our bubbles and so do our dogs.

I am not saying that we need to go back to the days of letting our dogs roam free because that would never do and is plainly ridiculous but we are in a situation where we need to work harder, focus more and plan more in order to ensure that our dogs get the chance to socialise responsibly, safely and effectively. It is one of the most important things any dog must learn to do and failure in this respect could become costly for you and a life sentence for your dog – it is that important.

Now that I have suitably frightened you then let me allay some fears and, as promised, dispel some myths about dog socialisation.

Let me start with myth number 1; if a dog is not socialised early it will always be unsociable and reactive? The short answer is no but, as you can imagine, this is too simplistic an answer. It is always recommended to let you puppy experience everything possible within the first 16 weeks of its life in order that it can experience and accept these as the 'norm' before it hits its first fear stage (5-8 months) and first rebellious period (6-12 months). However, it is not necessarily a disaster if it does not get the chance to be exposed to such experiences as much, or as often, as would be preferred. That being said, it can be a real challenge in later life if it did not, often or at all, experience the vast range of people interactions, dog interactions and different environmental situations during this vital development period.

If a dog does miss, or had missed, these valuable experiences within its socialisation window then you will need to take account of this and control and slow the exposure opportunities down in order to ensure that you keep your dog under its reactivity threshold. In such cases you should progress at a steady pace looking to make each (new) experience as positive as possible via treat, praise and play rewards. The aim is to build your dog's confidence when it is unsure of the new experience, reassure it that there is nothing to be concerned about and reward it for making the correct decision(s).

This may seem an obvious point but, worryingly, some dog experts do promote throwing a dog that has had limited social exposure right in at the deep end amongst other dogs/people and let it sort it out 'naturally'. These 'experts' call this 'immersion therapy' and, as you would expect, I would never support or recommend this type of 'therapy'. These strategies often fail and, in worst case scenarios, cause trauma, injury, damage or death. I will also guarantee that if you did choose this route that your dog will lose trust in you and it will be, almost certainly, traumatised in some way at the end.

If you do have a dog that has missed its opportunity to experience people and dogs within its socialisation period (8-16 weeks) then all is not lost and you just need to move onto a gradual introduction strategy going at your dog's pace not yours.

This leads me on to myth number 2; Your dog MUST socialise with all, or most, other dogs. Again, no. As I had said at the outset of this book dogs are as different and unique as you are and they have their own character traits and personalities. Some will be more inclined to interact and play with other dogs (i.e. Spaniels etc) but some will not (i.e. Staffordshire Bull Terriers etc) and you need to respect and work within their wishes. All dogs are different, even within the same breed.

Forcing a dog to interact is unfair and potentially cruel. Think about it in people terms. Some people are the life and soul of the party and thrive in meeting new people whereas other people like nothing more than a quiet meal for two and a trip to the theatre. Dogs are no different. In fact, I have found dogs to be either independent (task/job/function rewarded), people oriented or dog oriented and we should take stock of their propensities in order to get the best out of them and for them to get the best out of us.

The above being said, all dogs must have good social manners when meeting dogs or people irrespective of whether it is task, people or dog orientated. You may see a dog running around like a looney but in a fun-loving way at the dog park wanting to play with every dog or person it sees and think nothing of it. In fact, its guardian may also share this view and see it as doing no harm. But, and it is a big but (and I cannot lie…cheap joke I know), other dogs, and other dog guardians, may not see this as anything but unruly behaviour and react accordingly and, if I may say so, quite right too. I have absolutely lost count of the times I have heard "it's okay he is friendly and just wants to play" when a dog is coming at me, or my two dogs, at 100mph across the park. What the other dog's guardian seems to be forgetting is that it's rude, potentially dangerous, totally unacceptable and possibly law breaking. In the UK, and most US states, a person only needs to think that they are at risk from an unruly dog for it to be potentially classified as 'dangerous' irrespective of the intentions, obvious or otherwise, of the dog itself.

Again, from a common-sense perspective, would you want to play with the unruly and wild kid? Neither would I and neither would most dogs when it comes to ill-mannered dogs. It is just not acceptable and there are no excuses for this. If you do nothing more than to teach our dog to 'meet and greet' in an acceptable manner, as noted previously, then you will have already placed your dog ahead of the many other dogs I regularly see at dog parks etc.

Note: If your dog is not able, or ready yet, to be off lead and engage with other dogs and people in a socially acceptable way then it must stay on lead until it is, no exceptions.

There is another point of note here and, again, it is an important one to acknowledge and understand. Although your dog may not wish to play and/or interact with other dogs it MUST be able to be approached and be social and safe when interacting with other people. Even strangers. There is no defence for having a dog that is potentially unruly or dangerous to people.

As stated already, it is important to remember that people, if they feel at all concerned, can, and in my experience do, report dogs to the authorities even if an attack, or attempted attack, has not even taken place. A person just needs to feel threatened, in danger or view your dog as out-of-control (anti-social) to warrant a report to the local dog warden, or similar, and the law is on their side.

Myth number 3; It is only certain breeds that are considered dangerous dogs. No, this is incorrect as any dog is capable of aggression and attack. This is reflected in most dangerous dog legislation (US & UK) noting that it is not just the type (breed) of dog that is covered under the legislation even though certain breeds may be banned. For example, in the UK, under Section 3 of the

Dangerous Dogs Act, which was revised in 1997, it is an offence for an owner to allow his or her dog to be dangerously out of control in a public place, whatever the breed or "type", and this does not have to involve a dog attacking anyone. Being 'dangerously out of control' has been defined as: "any occasion on which there are grounds for reasonable apprehension that a dog will injure any person". Charges could therefore be brought against an owner even if his or her dog does not actually injure anyone.

In the US, although different US States have their own version of dangerous dog legislation basically, the universally accepted definition of a dangerous dog is a dog that without provocation, chases or menaces a person or domestic animal in an aggressive manner and/or causes injury to a person or other domestic animal.

I make no apologies for laying it on a bit thick in respect of sociability for dogs but I regularly experience the effects of the failure of this daily both in personal and professional contexts. It is all so unnecessary.

Myth number 4; a dog that 'air snaps' is aggressive or dangerous. Again, this is not necessarily the case and is another oversimplification. Firstly, a dog, in fact all dogs, must have the right, if its body signals are not being heeded and another dog still chooses to invade its personal space, to say 'no', 'enough' or 'too much'. Dogs will almost always give prior warnings like turning its head away, lip curling, baring teeth, moving away, growling etc before launching an 'air snap'. The 'air snap' is often the final warning that, if not heeded, may lead to the defending dog feeling that it needs to up the ante and actually make a contact bite with the agitator. Even then it is likely to be a soft bite that is not designed to cause injury but moreover designed to make it clear and obvious that the other dog has over-stepped the mark.

It is important to note that breed propensity does come into play here as some breeds just don't do 'soft bites' when their warnings are not being heeded and go into full scale attack mode. It is always best to be safe than sorry and intervene at the earliest sign of your dog showing you, or the other dog/person that it is uncomfortable. If you act then your dog does not need to.

The secret to avoiding these situations from arising is actually no secret. You must respect the warnings dogs give, every time all of the time. Dogs, in the main, do not want to attack or cause harm as this goes against the alliance traits that they have been bred for but if their warning signals are not being taken on board then it may feel the need to go to 'Defcon 2' and launch an attack. It is important to note however, if a dog really wants to cause actual damage it will do so as dogs have as deft a touch with the control of their mouth as we have with our hands. As stated, the air snap is the final warning before actual contact if all other body language (turning body or head away, lip curls etc) and vocal language (growling etc) warnings have gone unheeded. I actually consider it good dog manners for a dog to exhibit these warnings signs rather than just attack, therefore you would do well to respect it.

Dog play is often confused with dog fighting but although it is fast and rough it is often carefully judged (by the dogs) and consenting. What I mean by consenting is that the dogs will take it in turns to chase, or attack and then be chased or attacked. One dog may choose to self-handicap itself, especially if it is bigger or stronger than its play partner, to allow itself to be 'attacked' and will deliberately play soft when the roles are switched. Doggy play is just an enactment of its naturally predatory behaviour. If you don't see the switching, or one of the dog is trying to constantly get way, make itself small, being pinned down with no ability to get back up or yelping then the game is not 'equal' and needs to be stopped. Dogs can be bullies and be bullied too. Energy is another key ingredient in acceptable doggy play.

If any dog's energies significantly rise and play becomes evidently more 'forceful' then you will need to calmly break up the play and allow them to take a breath in order to reduce their energies again. In such situations you will often see the dogs perform a 'reset shake' (vigorous and rapid shaking of their head and top half of their body for a brief period) in order to release some of the built-up adrenalin and bring their own energies back down again. After this, they may choose to either resume play, go elsewhere or go rest.

I would also like to restate that the energy (again with the energy – sorry) of your dog is also a key factor that if your dog enters a park, even a dog park, like a coiled spring then this can potentially create a volatile atmosphere, potential conflict, and will make getting the attention and focus of your dog, should you need to, almost impossible. If your dog is amped up then it will be focused on everything else but you and may gorge on the play opportunity and become too full on. You should always ensure that you do your best to manage the energies of your dog and, in this respect, if your dog's energies are bouncing before you enter the park then I would not recommend entering the park. By entering a park when your dog is like a bouncing ball means that you are inadvertently rewarding uncontrolled energy and your dog will see no reason to change its behaviour going forward which, for me, is always a recipe for disaster.

Mental Stimulation

All dogs, irrespective of breed, need plenty of mental stimulation therefore you need to present both mental stimulation as well as physical exercise in order to satisfy their physical energy and cognitive intelligence requirements. Mental workouts for your dog will often satisfy breed tendencies and release feel good and relaxing hormones such as serotonin and endorphin. Also, as stated previously, game playing helps strengthen the bond between guardian and dog as well as increasing its focus, confidence and overall contentment whilst instilling or reinforcing life rules and boundaries.

As game playing can be mentally challenging for a dog and can be even more energy sapping than physical exertions, I recommend 'short-duration' training of approximately 5-10 minutes a couple, or several, times a day rather than lengthy sessions of half hour plus. This should keep games and training both fun and exciting for both you and your dog. You will not only end up with a well-balanced, enriched and wholly satisfied dog but also a dog that is looking forward to the next play opportunity. I believe that the famous mantra of always leave them wanting more is as true for dogs as it is for people.

I have noted below some games that can be played and the benefits thereof. This is not a comprehensive list but just indicative of games that can be played.

> **Game 1**: **Let's go hunting**: If you use dry food why not 'ditch the bowl' and scatter feed dinner a couple of times per week it will make feeding time into a game which, in my experience, dogs really enjoy, especially if they were originally bred to scent or hunt. Scatter feeding is simple. For best results I would recommend a smooth flat surface such as the kitchen floor or similar. Basically, instead of putting the dry food into a bowl for your dog to eat from you 'scatter' the food around the floor for your dog to 'hunt' and eat. Most dogs love this game.

Game 2: **Impulse control**: Impulse control is a great activity in order to help build control and restraint in your dog as well as reinforcing you as the resource provider. Further, to this if you have an always-on or hyper energetic dog then impulse training can go a long way in teaching your dog to slow down. That being said, I believe, that there are no dogs that would not benefit from impulse control training irrespective of breed or temperament.

To start, place a treat on the floor and 'protect' it with your hand as your dog will, quite naturally, look to get at it. As your dog realises it cannot get it the lift your hand slightly exposing more of the treat to your dog. If your dog moves forward to the treat the put your hand back and protect the treat again. There is no need for any instruction at this point.

Once you get to a point where you can raise your hand and your dog does not move forward then get it to wait a few seconds then point to the treat, say "go feed" (or similar) and take a small step back. Your dog should then go eat the treat (if not just guide it to the treat and re-issue the instruction "go feed").

Repeat the above until you get to the point where you can put the treat down and your dog does not any movement in order to try to get it. At this stage your dog should understand what is required and refrain from eating the treat until given the instruction to do so. From herein it is just practice.

Game 3: Playing fetch: If your dog has any interest in balls (or frisbee) then you can teach it to fetch, return and drop the ball/toy at your feet. This game is great for burning off excess physical energy before beginning training programs.

Step 1:   Get 2 tennis balls and place one behind your back and throw the other for your dog to chase.

Step 2:   When your dog comes back to you, before it has a chance to stop or move away, show it the other ball and then immediately throw that ball. Hopefully your dog will drop the original ball and chase the new ball.

Step 3:   Repeat this until your dog seems to drop the ball in expectation.

Step 4:   Once stage 3 happens introduce the command "drop" and carry on with the game as before.

Step 5:   Once this has been repeated several times your dog will learn that "drop" command means it must drop the ball.

Step 6:   Once at this stage and your dog consistently drops the ball then take this a stage further and get your dog to sit before throwing the ball again.

Step 7:   Repeat, repeat, repeat.

Game 4: **Kong play**: This is a great mental stimulation game. Pack the Kong tightly with some (slightly softened) dry food. You can place some peanut butter (that excludes xylitol (I am unable to recommend a particular brand just in case they change the formula but a good article to read on this is https://www.dfordog.co.uk/blog/peanut-butter-xylitol-danger-to-dogs.html)). Give the Kong to your dog and let it work out the food itself.

Just place the Kong on the floor in front of your dog then give it a command such as "go play", point to the Kong gesturing for your dog to go to it. Once this has been repeated several times over several days/weeks the command alone should be sufficient. The Kong should now focus your dog's attention for the next 15-20 minutes.

On the warmer days you can freeze the Kong overnight. Doing this will also keep your dog cool while it works away at the Kong. This is a great game to use as part of a program for dealing with separation anxiety etc. I will detail this more in the chapter 'common issues and challenging behaviour'.

This game is also great when you are sitting down to your own dinner/meal and your dog has a habit of begging or trying to table-surf to steal food or scraps.

Game 5: **Chase**: Place a ball/furry toy on the end of a piece of string. Play with the toy in front of your dog just to excite it to the point where it wants the toy. Then get your dog to sit, place the toy just a bit away from it (with you holding the top end of the string) and pull the string making the toy move and let your dog chase the toy.

This is a great game for not only sighthounds but also terrier and ratting breeds as it satisfies their core breed tendencies.

Game 6: Raggy: The key to productive and controlled raggy play is getting your dog to 'let go' on cue. Dogs grab things naturally but they don't let go naturally therefore they need to be taught to do so. This will mean that you, as the guardian, will control the game and not your dog. Your dog will enjoy the experience more if this is the case as the significant fun of this game is not only ragging the rope/toy but the engagement with you.

The important factor in achieving a good 'let go' response in your dog is to make the toy exciting when you want your dog to engage with the toy and make it boring when you want it to stop. To do this move the toy around your dog in a fast and frantic manner and couple this with high pitched exciting noises and as soon as your dog clamps down on the toy the vigorously move the toy left and right. Whilst you are doing this (ragging) maintain yourself in an excited and animated state in order to keep your dog interested.

Once you are ready to stop give a command such as "release" and stop all movement and sound but keep a hold of the toy. Initially your dog will not understand what the command means or why the game has stopped and will probably try to keep ragging. However, your dog will need to take a break and at that point, say nothing but quickly move the toy away and out of reach and out of sight of it.

After a couple of seconds quickly reintroduce the toy again in the same way you had done so previously and restart play. When you are ready to stop issue the release command and the stop all engagement but this time when you move the toy out of reach then immediately reintroduce it again in the above exciting and enticing manner.

Repeat the above several times and, soon, your dog will release the toy upon hearing the release command. What is happening here, in your dog's mind, is the game is not stopping when it hears the release command but it becomes a pre-curser for the toy being reintroduced in a fun and exciting way again. Even when you finally stop play your dog will still think, next time you play, that the 'release' command is the cue for fun and excitement with you.

Game 7: Go Rest: This is a great game that, once embedded, can help in so many situations (much as the 'look at me' exercise can).

Firstly, if you do not have a dog bed to use then try and use a mat or small rug. Place a treat on the dog bed and point to where it is and let your dog go and get it. Repeat this until your dog is expecting the treat to be on the bed. At this stage you can introduce the command "go rest" point to the bed and place the treat.

Your dog should now know to go to the bed to get a treat. Repeat this until you feel that your dog is starting to understand what the command 'go rest' means.

To test the effectiveness of the command then issue the instruction but don't point to the bed. If your dog moves to the bed to get the treat then great well done. If not, then just go back a step or two and repeat and test regularly until your dog does get it. It may take a bit of time but your dog will get there in its own time.

Once your dog responds correctly each time you issue the command then you can look to introduce distance. Introducing distance entails taking a step or two away from the bed and the issuing the command. Once your dog responds as you want it to at that distance then you can take further steps away and build to the point that you can issue the command from anywhere and your dog will go to the 'rest area/dog bed'.

Now that you can instruct your dog to 'go rest' you need to teach it to stay there until instructed to leave. In order to let your dog know that you have allowed it to leave the area you can issue a command (such as "leave") thus permitting your dog to come off the bed/rest area.

To achieve this, once your dog goes into the bed then immediately issue the leave command take a step back and lure your dog towards you with a treat. Once your dog gets to you then get it to sit and issue the praise and give it the treat (and praise) reward.

Once your dog starts to make the connection of the 'leave' command to the required action then you can introduce the 'stay' element. To do this, once your dog goes on the dog bed/rest area, take a slow step back. If your dog looks to move off the bed then issue the stay command and place your hand up in the 'stop' manner. If your dog then stops trying to move forward then continue your step back but, if it does still want to move off to you then you move forward to it reaffirming the 'stay' command and ensuring that your dog does not leave the rest area.

When you can get your dog to stay put reliably and consistently then you can take a further step or two back, then, after a short stay, issue the 'release' command, lure your dog to you, get it to sit for the reward.

From herein, all you do is increase the 'stay' duration and build the distance before issuing the 'release' command. Your dog should wait in situ for your 'release' instruction.

However, if at any stage your dog does move before you have given the release command then just send it back to the bed using the 'go rest' command and shorten the distance a bit before issuing the release command.

It may take a bit of time to become rock solid but once your dog gets it then it will be a great exercise for you to use in many different situations, such as when the door goes, visitors, when you are eating etc. This 'game' does require daily practice, even if your dog is getting it, in order to help the 'go rest' command become habit forming (habituated) in your dog.

You can also give your dog a Kong toy, chew toy or dental chew stick or such like for it to focus on to solidify your dog's desire to stay in the rest area.

Say No procedure: There may be times where you have to let your dog know that they need to immediately stop whatever they are doing and focus on, and listen to, you. In most situations I always promote the "don't think stop, think change" principle but sometimes, often for safety reasons, you will need your dog to immediately desist from what it is doing.

As with all training, practice this technique plenty of times before you need to apply it in order to stand the best chance of it working when you really need it to.

You can deliver the 'stop' technique by raising your hand (as if you are stopping a person, bike etc) and say "No" in a calm but assertive tone. There is no need to repeat this. You can, if you feel it more natural, add your dog's name to the end of the 'No' command.

If you get your dog's attention then immediately thereafter you can apply a sit command and reward it for doing so. As a variation, especially if you need your dog away from its current spot, you can say something like "come on <dog's name>" and guide your dog away then get it to sit (away from the original spot) and give it the reward.

If your dog does not pay heed to the 'No' command then take a step toward your dog and re-issue the command as above. For some dogs you may have to close down their space until you are almost standing over them to get the desired response.

Some dogs will get this straight away and others, such as beagles, may require a bit more time to get it but, if repeated often and consistently enough then your dog will eventually understand that "No" means stop what you are doing, look at me (or follow me) and listen.

Game 8: Choose a Toy: In this game you will teach your dog to retrieve the toy that you have asked it to retrieve.

> **Step 1**: Name this toy. Monosyllabic or disyllabic names work best as it is easier for your dog to pick out the 'sound' of the name from all of the other sounds that may be around.
>
> **Step 2**: Place the toy in front of your dog. When your dog shows some interest in it (preferably noses it) then let it know it has done well by saying something like "great" and then reward your dog. I have noted the word 'great' here but the word that you use is up to you but it just needs to be verbally comforting to your dog. This will be our 'well done' *marker sound*.

Step 3: Repeat step 2 until your dog automatically (proactively) explores the toy when you put it down. At this stage verbally announce the name you have given the toy just as your dog goes to explore it. Issue marker sound once it makes contact with the toy. However, this time, take a brief pause before you issue the reward.

Step 4: At this stage say the name of the toy, put the toy down and then wait until your dog explores it then issue the marker sound. Again, after a short pause issue the reward.

Step 5: Repeat step 4 until you are confident you can say the name of the toy and your dog will then investigate the nominated toy upon hearing the name you have given the toy. Now, assuming all is going well at this stage, you are ready to introduce a second toy. As before give this toy a unique name.

Step 6: Now remove the first toy and introduce the new toy. Repeat steps 2 – 5 with this new toy.

Step 7: Now, once your dog is responding consistently to the new toy then introduce both toys together. Once they are both in front of the dog name one of the toys and give the verbal marker if, or when, your dog investigates the 'named' toy. It does not matter just now if your dog does not go direct to the named toy just as long as you mark and reward your dog when it does do so.

Step 8: Keep this game going by randomly switching the name of the toy and marking and rewarding your dog when it chooses the correct toy.

Step 9: Now you can introduce a third toy. As before, name this toy and remove the other toys and repeat steps 2 – 5 with this new toy.

Step 10: Now introduce all three toys and repeat steps 7 and 8 both this time with 3 toys.

From herein, it is just practice and, if desired, adding more toys.

Game 9: Carry an Item: This is a great game that instils focus, patience and mental discipline in your dog.

For this game I would recommend using something fairly light, soft with no small bits or hard edges that your dog is not likely to destroy and swallow. Personally, I tend to use a ragging rope because I can use it for a variety of games after the 'carry'.

Firstly, you need to ensure that your dog is interested in the item. To achieve this make the item exciting to your dog by frantically moving it around in front of your dog whilst being animated and excited yourself. When your dog focuses on the item throw it down on the floor between you and the dog. You dog should now go to pick the item up. When it does pick up the he/she should, in most cases, look to return to you, even if they are not looking to give you the item. At this point, whilst still facing you dog, take a couple of steps back, wait for your dog to come to you and then show your dog a treat. Your dog should drop the item to get the treat. When giving the treat give plenty of praise. Repeat the above exercise to ensure that you dog picks the item and returns to you each and every time.

Now you need to increase the distance that your dog needs to 'carry' the item so this time when you throw down the item throw it a bit further away from both you and your dog and reward as before.

Keep repeating this exercise gradually increasing the distance each time you feel your dog has 'bagged it' at the distance you are currently working at. Once you get to a metre or two away from you and your dog then you can introduce the actual 'carry'.

The 'carry' element is where your dog will retain the item whilst walking alongside you. To achieve this, as before, throw the item down but this time issue the command "carry" (or similar) turn your back and slowly take two or three steps away. This time when your dog returns just keep on walking (slowly) for a few more steps then stop and reward your dog.

Now that you are increasing the distance and time between rewards you may need to give your dog mini rewards en-route to the main reward to retain focus. To do this just praise your dog as you walk but don't issue any treats.

Once you have managed to take 10 or so slow and steady steps then stop and reward. From herein it is just increasing the distance and practice. Before too long your dog will be walking alongside you and carrying the item in its mouth. The treat reward can be phased out but the praise retained.

Breed behaviour

Although not all breeds, nowadays, display their core breed behaviours and some dogs seem to display behaviours that are seemingly alien to their actual breed tendencies, it is important to ensure that you reward any natural inclination or instinct shown by your dog. This should be the case whether it is understood to be breed prevalent or not. Failure to do so may lead your dog to self-satisfy which often leads to unwanted and obsessive compulsive disorder (OCD) behaviours. It is always better to give your dog an outlet for a behaviour trait rather than try to inhibit such which, in my experience, often makes the situation worse.

If your dog has propensities' that it is driven to satisfy then it will not understand why it cannot do so. This is the case even if this is causing people issues. Breed satisfying game playing is a great way to allow controlled outlet for these drives and will lessen the compulsion for your dog to display these in undesired and unwanted ways.

Remember, dogs have been bred for specific roles and jobs such as guarding, herding, as sight hounds, water dogs, flushing, sledding, ratting and even companionship. Unfortunately, modern living no longer requires a lot of the behaviours that they were bred to perform. I personally believe that evolution is shaping out many core breed traits in domesticated dogs as the need for such is just not there anymore. However, if your dog does show a propensity for a behavior then it should be satisfied in some way. Dogs do not understand the reasons for not being able to act out the trait activity.

I do think, although I have absolutely no scientific proof for this, that breed bloodlines will, within six or seven generations, be sub-divided into 'working bloodlines' where a dog is truer to its core breed traits and 'domesticated bloodlines' where a dog may have breed tendencies but these are less prevailing and not as prominent.

To be safe and ensure that unresolved behavioural traits do not lead to any unwanted or destructive behaviours then if your dog is showing a propensity for any specific trait, or traits, then it is always wise to try to satisfy it rather than ignore or inhibit it.

Good outlets for satisfying such trait propensities are local agility, flyball, cannicross, doga clubs etc. These will not only allow your dog to access highly stimulating and potentially breed satisfying activities but, going to such clubs, is great for meeting and sharing information and tips with other guardians. These clubs can become great social outlets for you and your dog.

It does have to be said though, even noting all of the above, there is a small number of dogs who are not wholly play positive. Of course, 99.9% of dogs will want to be active to some degree and play (even if it is just in short bursts before they get fed up and stop), there is that very small, almost minute, community of dogs that just don't want to play no matter what. For them, comfort and companionship is THEIR valued currency. There is no issue with this per se, but you need to take care to ensure that they do not become lazy, over-weight or become over-attached to you.

That does not mean that they need to live a life without games or play. No, for these type of dogs activities such as impulse control and scatter feeding their meals (ditch the bowl) games are just the ticket. Such games are good as it allows them to enjoy a play outlet without this being overt or overly taxing. Although all dogs should earn their treats (give something to get something) it is even more pertinent for the less active dogs around. We should, however, take care not to smother them by giving them constant attention else they will become addicted to it and crave it 24/7. Attention and companionship, much alike games, need to be controlled and be part of a dog's balanced lifestyle in order to ensure it remains healthy, happy and fulfilled.

You can now understand the importance play has in a dog's world. If you choose not to afford your dog adequate mental and physical stimulation and enrichment then, chances are, the dog will look internally to satisfy any drive or compulsion it has which, if unfulfilled, often leads to problem behaviour. In fact, playing games regularly with your dog reduces the chances of your dog becoming unruly and out-of-control ten-fold, if not more. That being said, even if you do everything right there is not guarantee that your dog will respond as you would like. In the next chapter I will be covering common issues and behavioural challenges.

'ITS PLAYTIME' CHAPTER SUMMARY

- **Importance of play**
- **Mythbusting:**
  - **Dog socialisation**
  - **Air snaps**
- **Dog feedback**
- **Mental stimulation**
- **Games to play**
- **Breed satisfaction**
- **Dogs that do want to play**
- **Dogs that don't want to play**
- **Managing energy**
- **Breed tendencies**

Chapter 6: Common Issues and Challenging Behaviours

It is always interesting to me that we often look at the dog as doing something wrong when our dog displays behavioural issues. I know I have stated this already but the concept of right and wrong is alien when it comes to dog behaviour and is, at best, unhelpful but, at worst, counter-productive. If we can remove the premise of right and wrong altogether and work with the understanding that our dog is just displaying the behaviour it feels it needs to in order to satisfy an immediate compulsion then it will make it easier for us to view the situation from our dog's perspective.

It is also never wise to anthropomorphize displayed dog behaviour as you will be applying people rules to primal canine reasoning. It just does not work like that in a dog's world. It is always best to deal with what you know as fact and not to layer situations with unhelpful labels such as right, wrong, guilt etc.

It is also recommended, for the best results, is not to think 'stop' but instead think 'change'. Adopting this 'change' approach allows you to move from trying to inhibit undesired behaviour, which is really difficult (and often fails), onto promoting an alternative more desired behaviour. Basically, you are telling your dog "no you cannot do this but you CAN do this instead".

Humankind is naturally great at focusing on the negative and giving punishment rather than offering praise but, this does not work well for dogs and, in order to stand the best chance of achieving consistently successful outcomes, you would do well to reverse this philosophy.

It is also wise not to over-complicate matters or over think the reasons as to why your dog is doing what it is doing. You can often spend too much time and energy looking at the possible reasons why rather than trying to teach the new desired behaviours. If you do know, then fantastic, but if you don't then you can take a reasonable guess given what you do know but do take care to always deal with the facts rather than any (dog or human) emotion of the issue. Remember, from earlier in the book, successful poker players are consistent 'winners' even though they have to work with partial or imperfect information. It is always best to deal with what you do know and not try and second guess what you don't.

Preventative action or controlling the environment is, especially if you don't know the circumstances that preceded the issue (antecedent) is always going to stand you in good stead. If you can possibly look to managing the environment that triggers the unwanted behaviour then you could reduce, or even stop, the unwanted behaviour from arising in the first place.

It also important to psychologically place yourself in the footsteps (paw steps) of your dog and how it views the world around it. If you have a care-free and naïve dog that sees the world as a playpark then this is not so much of an issue. If, however, for whatever reason, your dog is not sure about the environment or its place in the current environment, then you need to take this into consideration and look to slow things down greatly and build up its confidence via games, especially mentally challenging games where you dog needs to learn decision making. This is an issue that I come across a lot when dealing with 'rescued' or 'rehomed' dogs as they may not have enjoyed positive, or even stable, support right up until the point that they have come into your world. This is also an issue for 'runt of the litter' pups who have had to fight to get food or attention with its litter-mates and just views the world as one big battleground.

At this point I would also like to say a bit about mood. Just as mood can affect us as humans the same is also true of dogs. A dog can 'get out of bed on the wrong side' just the same as we can. Dogs are not emotionally static beings where you will be guaranteed the same mood day in and day out. Yes, they are less prone to mood swings, but unlike us they are generally more stable in their mood (character) most days but, unfortunately, this can never be guaranteed. So, if you think your dog is just not in the mood for something then, chances are, you are correct. At that point you can either stop or change what you are doing or increase the rewards on offer to elicit motivation.

Before I go any further in this chapter, I would like to dispel the 'bad dog' myth. I don't believe any dog, even those with psychological imbalances, is bad or wants to be bad. Unless trained to, or via actual negative experience(s), dogs do not enjoy conflict and only look to engage with other dogs or people as part of its self-protective last resort. That being said, some dogs, especially guarding bred dogs, may enjoy the adrenalin rush and outcome if allowed to fight which, if experienced, could become a 'learned response' therefore, in future, a default response position. However, this is rare. Most dogs engage in acts of aggression, or actual fights, via fear and see such a response as their last and only option in order to see off the cause of the fear.

Dogs are as unique as we are and have much the same range of character traits that we do minus the social or moral complexities that we have as people. As with people, some dogs are more social in nature and others not so much. Some dogs are more compliant in nature whereas others may be more defiant. This does not make them good or bad but, moreover, makes them unique.

Another myth I wish to bust is that there are 'bad breeds' as this is total nonsense. Firstly, a dog breed has been bred for a purpose and no purpose I know of includes being bad. Even so-called banned breeds are not bad but have been bred to have more confidence going into conflict situations than other dogs and may actually learn to enjoy the adrenalin rush of conflict if allowed to experience such. For the record, just to be absolutely clear, I do not support breed specific legislation as, for me, it totally misses the point and it is bad guardianship other than bad dogs, that causes the majority of issues.

Often it is the type of person that is drawn to certain breeds that is the real issue here. I am totally a-political but, for me, this does need to be addressed via better government and agency support, general (community) dog guidance and swift corrective actions by the protective agencies for the safety and security of both people and dogs. Dogs are being punished and stigmatised due to the fact that legislation fails to address the real reasons for dog attacks and dog aggression etc. This is dog (and breed) ignorance plain and simple.

Furthermore, as noted already in this book, some dogs are truer to their breed traits whereas in others this is hardly evident at all. You can get two dogs of the same breed, even from the same litter, and they could have totally different trait characteristics and personalities (temperament). This is even more pertinent in the modern world as few dogs actually get to do the job they were originally bred for. In fact, it is not bad breeds we need to be concerned with but, instead, as stated, bad guardians. A dog is often a mirror of its home or living environment.

Dogs are less sociable now which directly reflects the fact that we, as people, are also less sociable now. You no longer have communities in the true sense of the word and you no longer, or rarely, see dogs roaming freely in the streets. This is all so different to when I was growing up. We now tend to live our lives at arms length from each other within our own social bubbles and interact remotely (online) or, at best, infrequently face-to-face. Modern living has not helped our dogs at all. Remember, these dogs were originally 'bred' for purpose and also to be socially interactive animals. Dogs are social animals and are hard wired to 'crave' interaction, especially with people. We have got to a point where we need to, even more so than before, teach our dog how to be social and interact correctly with both people and dogs whereas, previously, they did not need our guidance as much and relied more on learning by osmosis.

This situation is recognised and has led to the introduction, and growth, of dog parks, dog sitters, dog walkers and dog day care centres. Just 10 years ago, especially in the UK, these would have been unheard of.

As good teachers and guardians we need to help our dogs adjust to modern living as almost every aspect of our brave new world is alien and regressive to our dogs and their wellbeing. This is not a comment or criticism but rather a statement of fact and the canvas from which we need to understand and work from.

With the above in mind I will now present some common behavioural issues and proposed solutions in order to overcome these. As with everything I promote, these are only listed as frameworks and it is important that you adapt the principles and key points of these programs to match the character (traits), temperament (energy) and personality (optimist/pessimist) of the dog you have.

Setting the development foundation

Before you can begin trying to modify any behavioural issues you need to establish a development baseline in order to ensure that you afford your dog the best chance of success. What we do not want to do is set up our dog to fail. To this end I have developed the **PERFECT** method of setting a solid foundation to enable behavioural modification success.

This method will allow you to set, manage and get into the right mindset to help you plan and deliver your desired doggy development program. Adopting this method will not only ensure that the training you do deploy gets the results you want but that it is also <u>rewarding</u> for both <u>you and your dog</u>. The latter point is crucial.

<u>The acronym PERFECT stands for</u>: -

<u>P</u>repared: When training, especially at the initial stages, you should ensure that the training environment is safe and distraction free or, at the very least, distraction controlled. Set realistic objectives. Don't look for, or expect, too much too soon because, if you do, chances are you are setting up for failure and nobody wants that. Set the training duration. By keeping sessions short and interesting but frequent you will maintain the interest, focus and engagement from your dog. Without this, even with the best plan in the world, your training is doomed.

Ensure that any program maintains the dog under its reactivity threshold. The last thing you want is to fight for your dog's attention and focus when it is in an emotional state and focused on something else, either good or bad, other than you. Finally, ensure you have the rewards in place that you know will resonate with your dog. The value of the reward is key especially if the behaviour you want is competing with behaviour your dog itself prefers to exhibit. If this is the case then you will need to, ideally, get your dog away from what it is reacting to and ensure that the rewards you have on offer adequately incentivize your dog to focus on you and not anything else.

Energy (Eyes on you): I have mentioned this aspect consistently throughout this book but it is vital that your dog is calm and focused on you. If your dog is amped up or like a coiled spring before you begin training then you are really going to struggle to achieve any type of success. It is always recommended you allow your dog to expend some energy via play or a walk before you begin and training session.

Your energy is also important as most dogs are very energy sensitive therefore you need to ensure that you are in a calm but assertive (not aggressive) mood. By deploying the 5 Cs (calm, confident, controlled, consistent and concise) you will ensure that your guidance will resonate with your dog. It will be problematic if you and your dog have mis-matched energies and your dog's focus is not on your instruction but your emotion. Bear in mind dogs are expert people readers and can almost telepathically read our emotions and intent and you need to be acutely cognisant of this.

Your dog should also be incentivized to look at you as its default position because if it is not looking at you how can you teach it?

Rewarding: Basically, you need to understand what, from your dog's perspective, it should respond in the way you want it to. You will need to satisfy the 'what's in it for me?' question and ensure that your reward is more appealing than other temptations that may be around. If you view rewards as currency then sometimes you will need to pay $1 and other times, $5 to get the focus on you. It all depends on what other incentives or interests are around that may seem more tempting to your dog than anything you that have to offer.

Focused: Eye contact is crucial. You will need to ensure that not only are your dog's eyes are on you but, equally, your eyes are on it. Remember learning is a two-way process. You will be surprised how well you will get to know and learn about your dog just via observation. Not only this, if your attention does wander, your dog will pick up on this and do likewise.

Engaging: You need your dog to want to take notice of you therefore your tone and actions need to be interesting and exciting to it. If you want to incentivise action the raise the energy but if you want to let your dog know they have not quite achieved what you want or even if you show disapproval then do so by lowering your energy and remaining calm and in control.

A quick note on showing disapproval, positive reinforcement training does not mean that you cannot let your dog know that you don't approve, especially when it comes to negative behaviour modifying, as that would be ridiculous. In the dog world dogs will create space (turn their head away, move away etc) when they do not approve. You can replicate this via the 'dynamic silence'. Although this may seem a bit counter-intuitive, when using dynamic silence, try not to verbally correct your dog (by saying something like "stop" or "no" etc (unless of course you have to for control or safety reasons). Instead stand still, look into the distance and say nothing. If your dog is focused on you, as it should be, then it will try and appease you, as dogs don't like silence, or disengagement. Your dog may go through an appeasement repertoire (sitting, giving a paw etc) none of which was unrequested by you, in order to re-engage with you.

A few seconds after you feel your dog has exhausted its appeasement repertoire then give your dog a sit (or lie down) command and, when it complies, give it plenty of praise and, if appropriate, a treat. You are now back in control and can progress accordingly.

If your dog is not focusing on you then you can always turn your back, create distance but still refrain from any verbal engagement with your dog. Hopefully, your dog will not like the distance you are creating, or will get curious, and come over to you. If so, get your dog to sit (I call this a compliance sit) then reward it and re-engage.

You will also want to ensure that your body language is calm, assertive and congruent with your verbal delivery as any mixed signals from you will confuse your dog and lessen the strength of the engagement between you both.

One thing to remember is that, when withdrawing engagement, we are not only giving our dog 'reflection' time but also time to decompress and reduce any energy built up via its frustration. Giving a dog time to decompress is vital and often overlooked when it comes to dog training. It is often not very productive or effective to try and teach, or guide, a dog that is in a highly emotional or energetic state therefore allowing time for this to reduce naturally will be so rewarding for both you and your dog.

Finally, don't try to do too much too soon which may potentially confuse or frustrate your dog. Adopt the KISS (Keep It Session Simple) approach to all things training. The best training successes are when the response elements have been broken down into small steps and built up slowly piece by piece. Trying to do everything at once, or too quickly, rarely works and will no doubt just leave both you and your dog tired, frustrated and no further forward.

Confident: It is human nature to err on the side of caution and, as such, we tend to focus on negative outcomes by default. Normally this would serve us (humans) well but when it comes to dog training it is counter-productive. We know dogs are super intuitive and can sense things at an almost telepathic level. This is normally good but can allow fear transference to occur whereby your dog is on alert because you are on alert. When you tense up, tense the lead, or change your behaviour, even in a very small, almost subliminal, way, because you may be concerned that something may go wrong or you are readying yourself from a perceived negative outcome then you send out signals to your dog. Unfortunately, by doing so you are in danger of creating the actual issue/conflict and thus allowing your prophecy to materialise.

Dogs can also smell the chemical changes in your body and smell your fear or emotional change. It can, unless understood and acknowledged, easily become an ever-decreasing circle. To combat this you should keep your body language loose and relaxed as much as possible and stick to the 5 Cs. I know that it can be hard at times but if you can maintain the calm assertiveness that we know dogs respond to then the success of your training endeavours will benefit greatly.

Timing: This element is key to your success. More often than not you will wish to 'mark' the good behaviour as soon as it occurs, by saying "good" or "great" etc, to let your dog know it has done well. However, when dealing with issues such as unrelenting barking or dog reactivity, best results will arise if you can pre-empt the behaviour and get your dog calm and under your control again before you issue any 'mark' or 'reward'. If you try to correct your dog when it is in the middle of barking or reacting to something then you may inadvertently actually be encouraging more of it by, in your dog's mind, rewarding its actions.

Further, you need to be aware of correction/reward windows whereby the timing of your approval marker (sound) needs to be delivered within 1-3 seconds of the action in order for your dog to effectively link the sound (marker) coming from you to the action it has just completed. This does not mean that you need to give the dog a treat within this window but you do need to audibly 'mark' your approval within this period. The delivery of the treat can follow on many seconds after the marker, if it all.

Although timing is crucial if you do miss this marker window then don't worry and don't issue the reward but just repeat the exercise giving you and your dog a new reward window opportunity.

The timing element may sound like a bit of a minefield but it is not really. If you can remember that 'requested' behaviours, if responded to by your dog correctly, should always be marked asap, whereas 'reactive' behaviour should, where possible, be pre-empted and redirected away from the action or reaction trigger (stimulus) and only then be marked and rewarded (when your dog is calm and focused on you).

Reflect & Review

To progress effectively in any training endeavours you should remember to always review the highs and lows of your training. Be critical but don't be judgemental as this will neither help you or your dog. In some cases, your training will excel but in others your training will need to take a step back. The key to training success is making small steps regularly rather than big steps irregularly. The sessions have not only to be productive but, more importantly, they need to be fun interlaced with plenty of rest periods. In any review you should be asking yourself the following: -

- Did your dog make any progress today? If yes, fantastic. If not, think back to the last step where you were successful and use this as the starting point for the next session.
- Was it enjoyable?
- Was your dog focused on you throughout?
- Was the chosen reward a good enough motivator? (Did you satisfy your dog's WIIFM (what is in it for me))?
- Was the training duration too long, too short or just right? (try and leave your dog wanting more therefore it should be more motivated to engage from the off in the next session)
- Did you manage to use the 5 Cs effectively?
- Did you give your dog options (i.e. teaching your dog what it CAN do rather than what it CANNOT)?

- Did you display positive patience (allowing your dog to make mistakes without criticism or emotional strain)?
- What went well?
- What did not go so well? (can you, or should you, change the training program or style of delivery in the future to combat this)?
- Have you scheduled the next training time/date?
- Have you set the objectives for the next training session?

In order to ensure that the PERFECT method is giving the best chance of success you need to set some boundaries for your dog to ensure that even out with structured training there are rules in place which your dog needs to adhere to. You can do this via the 'learn to earn' principles which I would recommend should be adopted as a way of life.

Learn to Earn:

Dogs need structure and routine to ensure that they feel safe and secure. If they know what is going on or what is likely to happen then they can ready, or set, themselves up to be able to deal with it. In order to have structure and routine then we need to have rules. The rules, however, is not a metaphor for being strict but, instead, being consistent. In the doggy world we call these 'boundaries'. Boundaries are the relationship rules that you have put in place to keep your dog safe, secure and well behaved. All dogs need boundaries. These boundaries (rules) are not, and should not be,

Draconian. Remember, you need your dog to trust in you in order to learn from you. Boundaries you set should support the bonding process and not become a barrier to it. 'Learn to Earn' is a great method for helping to establish boundaries and the acceptance, from your dog, of you setting the (life) rules.

Treats, praise and even attention are valuable resources for dogs. As part of the 'learn to earn' program your dog, in order to receive one, or more, of these it is recommended that you should only reward it when responding to an instruction from you. Your dog gets something when it gives something.

You should not 'reward' your dog when it demands something. This may seem obvious but it is not uncommon for guardians to reward their dog when it has made the decision to do something and not the guardian. Let me explain, an example of a demand is when your dog performs an unrequested action, such as giving a paw, nudging you, pawing you, etc in order to try and get you to give it a desired reward (i.e. attention, praise, treat). By rewarding these un-requested behaviours, you will be teaching your dog that there are exceptions to the rules (boundaries) and that it, rather than you, can instigate a reward response any time it likes.

In order to establish solid behavioural boundaries, the 'learn to earn' program will teach and remind your dog that you are the resource provider and you will control access to when and where your dog will be rewarded. There should be no exceptions to this as your dog will, as will all dogs, look to exploit 'exceptions' and thus will lessen the effectiveness of obtaining consistent compliance from your dog going forward. You do need solid compliance from your dog as you may be training a new behaviour or even looking to change an undesired behaviour to a desired one. It is important to remember that you are not punishing your dog but merely setting up some rules to ensure that it will get rewarded when it complies with your requests and not when it decides to make its own request (demand).

For the best results, I wholly recommend that the above needs to be adopted by all, whether they be family, friends or visitors. If everybody does the same then this will teach your dog that we, as people, are consistent, and that the requested/required responses are to be performed for all people and not just a select few.

Another positive of the learn to earn principle is that your dog will learn to manage its own energy and control more effectively and, as a positive consequence, reduce its adrenalin release making it a more stress-free, calm, attentive and content dog. It is important to note here that it is accepted that, on average, a consistently/constantly stressed dog will reduce its life span by approximately 2 years. Given this we have a duty of care to ensure that we provide as stress-free life as possible to our dog. Some stress, as with people, is good but regular, or high level, stress is not. We, as people, can deal with our stress via talking therapies but dogs cannot therefore it is always something that we should be mindful of and manage appropriately. In addition, stressed dogs are often more reactive and destructive dogs, requiring a lot more time and support than more balanced dogs.

On the subject of duty of care, as you are now on the chapter focusing on problem behaviour you need to adopt a safety-first approach to helping your dog and good control and management is fundamental in this regard. What I mean by this is that you need to ensure that you do not expose your dog, other dogs, other people or yourself to unnecessary risk. Not only should you always endeavour to work just under your dog's reactivity threshold, where behaviour anticipation is the best intervention, and build slowly therein but you need to ensure that nobody is put at risk or are put in the position where they FEEL that they are at risk. This is especially the case if you have a reactive dog. If this is the case, then you should always try to deliver training within a controlled and secure environment ensuring that your dog has no ability to cause fear or harm to anybody or anything. This is called **control and management** and it is important that you do everything you possibly can to ensure that you set your dog up for success and not failure.

Firstly, we need to ensure that we don't try to train in situations or circumstances that we know our dog will adversely react to. The main premise of positive reinforcement training is to gradually increase your dog's exposure to negative things to ensure that, as best you can, keep it under its full reactivity threshold. The key to success here is for your dog to notice and acknowledge the (perceived) 'threat' but then to be redirected away from it onto somewhere neutral and more pleasant. You are looking to change the relationship your dog has with the negative trigger (stimulus) to one that is more positive, if not, actually enjoyable. This is called counter-conditioning and is the fundamental principle of positive reinforcement training. Given this, you need to ensure, as best you can, that you control the environment to ensure that you are able to protect your dog, and yourself, from all foreseen negative triggers.

I do wholly understand that, in the real world, the above is not always possible and accidents can, and do, happen and you dog may go into full reactivity mode due to something out with your control. If this does happen the key for you to remain calm, guide your dog away and, once you are both at a suitable (non-reactive) distance then get your dog to sit with full focus on you and then mark and reward it. If you do unfortunately react to a negative situation with the same energy and vigour as your dog then you will be reinforcing your dog's response and it will look at your response as being the correct response and continue with its (negative) behaviour. This is why the 5 Cs are so important and should not be restricted just to training and development but moreover the general way of life.

Secondly, you need to ensure that your training endeavours are safe for you, your dog and other people. So, to this end, you should use such training tools as long leads, muzzles, hi viz etc. It does appear that one of the seemingly most contentious control and management safety precautions that can be taken is to muzzle our dog. This should not be the case and if you see a dog that is muzzled do not think 'dangerous dog' but instead think 'responsible guardian'. The dog could be muzzled for a variety of reasons with biting being just one. For example, a muzzled dog could be a dog that likes eat/graze anything and everything up from the ground so, to ensure that the dog does not swallow something dangerous, the guardian has applied a control and management precaution to, hopefully, stop this from happening.

For some people, no matter what, there is a stigma regarding muzzling their dog as they feel that if they do muzzle their dog then it gives other people the impression that their dog cannot be controlled. However, as stated, the opposite is true. Muzzling your dog is the responsible thing to do especially if there is any risk at all of your dog wishing to lunge and make mouth contact with someone, or something, else, irrespective if it wants to attack or play. Doing this lets everyone know that you put the safety of them and your dog at the heart of your development and training endeavours.

Remember, your dog is learning and finding its way and you are protecting it from doing harm or being reported. Further to this, if I am keeping myself and my dog safe, then I really do not care what other people may think. Personally, I would prefer to see a dog muzzled coming up to me than an over-exuberant (playful?) unmuzzled dog. A bite from an over-energised playful dog is still a bite and can hurt every bit as much.

You can always view a muzzle as a temporary training tool which, for me, is a positive addition rather than a negative one and will make for a happier training relationship. I have detailed below a step by step guide in how to 'muzzle train' your dog in order that not only does it accept the muzzle but it actually looks forward to it. This works because you will be teaching your dog that when it gets the muzzle on then good, if not great, things happen. If we were to suddenly introduce a muzzle, which is, lets be honest, a restrictive item for a dog, without preconditioning it to it then not only will your dog hate it but you will also learn to hate it too due your dog's reaction to it. The steps below will create a positive relationship between the muzzle and your dog.

Step 0. This is a foundation step. The aim here is to just to allow your dog to acknowledge the presence of the muzzle by having the muzzle nearby but with neither you or your dog focusing on it. Throw a treat on the floor for your dog but throw it a bit away from the muzzle. Next throw the treat a bit closer to the muzzle but not too close. Do the same again but this time a bit closer. Now reset and throw a treat to the place you threw the first treat then, again, another treat slightly closer to the muzzle and finally even closer to the muzzle as before. Each time taking care not to pay any attention to the muzzle.

Step 1. Now just lift the muzzle and let your dog see the muzzle directly but at a bit of a distance and give him/her a treat/praise then put it away.

Step 2. Repeat step 1 but each time move the muzzle very slightly closer to your dog (ensuring that he/she remains calm and happy for you to do so).

Step 3. Repeat the above until you can (lightly) touch your dog's nose with the muzzle and then move it away again and give him/her the reward. If you can do this repeatedly without your dog moving away or reacting negatively then you can introduce a command "muzzle" whilst you give him/her the treat.

Step 4. Repeat step 3 but this time issue the command, then touch your dog's nose with the muzzle and then issue the reward.

Step 5. Assuming all good up until this point then issue the command, place the muzzle gently at the tip of his/her nose (as if you were going to put it on its nose), move it away again and give him/her the reward.

Step 6. Repeat step 5 until you can lightly put the muzzle all the way on his/her nose but don't clip it and remove it after a few seconds.

Step 7. Repeat step 6 but increase the duration on his nose before you remove it and give him/her the reward.

Step 8. Once you get to about 30 seconds with no reaction then gently clip together the muzzle, unclip it immediately and remove the muzzle then reward your dog.

Step 9. Repeat step 8 but increase the duration (muzzle clipped) before removing it and rewarding your dog.

Step 10. Once you get to about 30 seconds or so with no adverse reaction from him/her then keep the muzzle on and give him/her a treat (or treats) through the front of the muzzle. There is no need to remove the muzzle just now just wait a few seconds more, issue the command "muzzle" and reward him/her again through the front of the muzzle. Once you have done this 3 times remove the muzzle, take a break and then start over again.

Step 11. Once you get to this stage your dog should have pretty much accepted the muzzle and you will now need to build on his/her positive experiences to it. To do this you should start positively interacting with him/her while he/she has got the muzzle on (playing games, doing some training etc) which should embed his understanding that the wearing of the muzzle means good things happen. Once you have stopped the interaction/play then unclip the muzzle and let him/her reflect on the fact muzzle on equals fun and muzzle off means fun ends.

Step 12. Once he/she has accepted the muzzle then (pre-walk) put the muzzle on your dog and then go through the pre-walk routine and go for a brief (minute or two) walk and the return home Once you get back in. Get your dog to sit, remove the muzzle, then give him/her a treat then proceed to remove the lead etc.

Note: Although <u>you</u> can take all of the precautions for <u>your</u> dog other guardians you may come across might not be as responsible as you and may have an uncontrolled dog off-lead (or sometimes even on lead) bounding about all over the place. If this is the case then you just need to manage the situation and create distance, body block or lift up your dog. There is little to be gained by trying to reason with the other guardian as they clearly have no idea of basic dog etiquette and you will be creating conflict with no feasible positive outcome. Further, they are seemingly happy to put their own dog at risk of attack, injury or even involvement from the dog authorities so it is unlikely that they will take sage feedback from you.

Now that you have set up the <u>foundation</u> for training and understand the more optimum styles of communication delivery I will list below some of the most common problem behaviours and detail some solutions frameworks. Again, as noted previously, these are not prescriptive but will provide a platform from which you can adapt in order to better suit you, your dog and your environment.

Talk with Purpose
For most of us humans verbal conversation is the main form of communication. For dogs it is the <u>last</u> form of communication. A dog focuses on the tone, pitch and resonance of the sounds that are emitted which it then relates, either automatically (classical conditioning) or by choice (operant conditioning), to an experience. Although some dogs are capable of picking out key (command)

sounds intermingled within other sounds (i.e. within your conversation) not all dogs can do this, it is inconsistent, unreliable and, more importantly, you cannot be 100% sure of exactly what 'command' your dog is actually responding to. Therefore, given this, you need to ensure that your vocal communication can be received by your dog loud and clear.

You need to remember that you are in a training and development period. For example, if I can relate this to going to a seminar on a subject that I have a keen interest in and the speaker then starts to chat about her breakfast that morning then, as it does not relate to the subject area, I will have a tendency to switch off and let my mind and focus wander. I would imagine you would do likewise. Dogs suffer from ADHD and don't have the attention spans that we do therefore, to ensure that your communication to them is not wasted then you should 'talk with purpose' in order to stand the best chance of your 'message' landing. What this means is that if you can restrict all unnecessary dialogue with your dog then this will ensure that any instruction you wish to deliver will be clear, defined and will not be lost within other actual dialogue.

We, as people, have a natural tendency to laden our dialogue with emotion, whether we are aware of it or not, running the risk of creating an 'event' (drawing attention to) a trigger/stimulus which could potentially raise your dog's anxiety. Dogs do tend to mirror our emotional state. For maximum control and influence everything should be 'low and slow' with focus being on the 5 Cs. This will reassure your dog that you have got everything in hand and that it does not have to worry about anything at all.

In addition to the above, adopting the teacher style of communication allowing your dog to make its own choices knowing it will be rewarded for the correct choice will enable it to not only 'own' the choices it makes but it will also increase its confidence and self-reliance in its decision making. In my experience, fear and lack of confidence is often a significant factor in reactive dogs, so allowing your dog to learn via positive experiences will not only strengthen its own decision making capabilities but also its confidence in doing so. Allowing your dog to positively learn from the choices it makes will enable the rewarded behaviour to be 'incentivised' to repeated and, in time, embedded. It is important, for dogs to feel secure, that they are able to make choices confident in the knowledge, from previous experience, that these will be rewarded but, importantly, none of which will be punished.

It is important to note though that dogs, as do people, need space in order to reflect and absorb information and outcomes therefore you should allow 'silence' to become a part of the training communication program. This, as previously noted, is called *dynamic silence* and it is not a passive characteristic as it allows both you, and your dog, adequate space to reflect, learn, absorb and adopt or adapt. There should be no rush to the finish line.

When you 'talk with purpose' you will tend to manage the energy of the communication. It is for this reason I have paid big attention to the energy in dogs, and dog training, as it is such a crucial factor. A dog that is 'always on' (high energy low focus) will be unproductive and many of them will, no doubt, tend to suffer from one, or more, behavioural issues due to its own poor energy management.

Given all of this I will now outline some solutions for common behavioural issues. Remember these are, in the main, generic and it is always recommended to take a flexible approach and adapt these to both your own, and your dog's, circumstances, character and contexts.

1. Jumping Up/Demanding Attention

Remember, we have bred dogs to be social animals and, because of this, it should come as no surprise that our dogs want to be with us and, because of this, greet us with excitement, pleasure and enthusiasm. That being said however, a dog jumping up is not just a case of over-excitement but it is also a 'demand' for attention and attention and/or interaction is a valuable resource which should always be governed by the guardian and not the dog.

It is also not acceptable for a dog to be jumping up on people, especially small children, therefore you need to teach your dog what is, and what is not, acceptable. There are several ways to achieve this.

Firstly, lets look at this from the dog's point of view people entering the room. Although this is a normal and natural activity for us humans, to a dog it is often a cause for either concern or excitement. Added to this very often, when we enter the home or a room, the very first thing we do is engage excitedly with our dog. For us, there is nothing like coming home to someone who is so super excited to see us and is more than happy to show it!

The problem here is that, by allowing this and giving your dog our attention from the minute you enter the room, you are rewarding your dog by giving it exactly what it is looking for. You are inadvertently reinforcing your dog's excited response and, if regularly repeated, this will become a learned behaviour and will become habituated (normalised) if not corrected. Once a behaviour is habituated it becomes, in your dog's mind, part of its life rules and an outcome expectation which will be deemed as normal and acceptable to your dog, whether you like it or not. Importantly, if you have a puppy then, no matter how small and cute it is, you should always set the rules from the off and, because you are starting out the way you wish to go on, your dog will accept these as the norm and part of its own life rules. Remember, that your dog will (probably) not be small forever and you will be amazed at how rapidly they will grow.

To counter this, the first thing you need to do here is, as hard as this will be, not to give your dog any attention when you enter or leave the home, or a room. No touch, no talk and no eye contact. The aim here is to reduce, or remove, the over-excitement of the process of walking in or the stress (to your dog) of walking out. To achieve this you need to enter and leave the room (or home) paying absolutely no heed to your dog. You need to ensure that when you enter, or leave, a room, or the house, you do not highlight the <u>emotion</u> and <u>energy</u> of this (significant to your dog) event by interacting with your dog and creating an emotional 'event'. The aim here is to nullify the emotive aspect of this activity.

It is of crucial importance that you pay as much importance to this principle when leaving and, as you do when you enter, do so without fuss or engagement with your dog. This, when repeated over time, will solidify the fact to your dog that any comings and goings are nothing at all to get excited about. If people do come and go and your dog is getting nothing interesting from these 'events' then the emotion and/or anxiety of doing so will be lessened, if not removed, and your dog will focus on something else instead. That particular 'something else to focus on' could be one, or more, of the suggestions below.

a. **Request an alternative response**: The key to this is to reward 4 paws on the floor and not 2 paws jumping up. This is my preferred option. If a dog has 4 paws on the floor then, by default, it cannot be jumping up.

To achieve this, when people come into the room/home, then you need to issue the sit (or lie down) instruction and reward compliance with the appropriate level of currency. The currency reward needs to be worth the effort, in your dog's mind, of restraining itself from the reward of jumping up. Of course, this will work much better if you have trained in a solid sit response already (as noted in the core training section).

To ensure that your dog does this when people enter the room we need to set up the scenario and practice. Initially if you practice this with yourself (issuing the instruction directly to your dog when you enter the room) and gradually extending this slowly to include everyone else within the house. By doing this bit by bit and building this up person by person then you will have a greater chance of success over trying to do this with everyone right from the off. Once you, and your family, can come and go without your dog's energies being raised and you are all able to get solid (compliance) 'sit' response then you can start to practice with guests etc. At this point your dog will be cued to sit, or expect the sit command, by the actual event of someone entering the room/home.

b. **Disapproval**: If obtaining a compliance sit is not getting the results you are looking, or your dog's energies suddenly rise, then you can show your disapproval, in a positive way, of this boisterous and undesired behaviour. Dogs tend to show their disapproval with each other by creating distance and turning their attention elsewhere leaving the other dog to reflect on its actions. You can, when showing your disapproval, do likewise by leaving the room when your dog's behaviour as not as you would like. When leaving you should take care not to engage or look at your dog as you leave (as this will, in your dog's mind, maintain the engagement and reduce the effect of you leaving the room). The aim here is to give your dog some pause, or paws, for reflection as to why you got up and left.

Note: For this to be effective everybody needs to leave the room else the point will be missed.

Close the room door over and wait 5-10 seconds then re-enter. If your dog resumes the undesired behaviour upon re-entry then immediately repeat the exercise and get everyone to leave the room again. However, if the dog is calm then continue to enter the room ensuring that no talking, eye contact or touching is made with the dog. Once you, and/or everyone is settled, then he/she can be called over for some attention, play and cuddles. You are rewarding the calm in this exercise and your dog will, eventually, work this out.

c. **Go rest**: Instruct the dog to "go rest" see game 7 in the 'its playtime' chapter. Again, it is recommended that you train this initially when it is only yourself, or possibly one other, entering the room and then work to gradually increase the numbers thereafter.

d. **Say no!**: As in game 7, I have noted a 'saying no' as a procedure. This is because you are not trying to punish your dog but, instead, you are teaching it what is not acceptable and, hopefully, re-directing it to something that IS acceptable. This action will let your dog know that you are not happy in a positive and supportive way and that its current behaviour is not acceptable. Once you get the focus from your dog then you can settle it down, via a compliance sit or similar, and thereafter redirect it to do something else more approving.

e. **Disengage**: Another technique you could use, should your dog decide it wants to get excited again, is to cross your arms, turn your back and look away thus giving the dog no interaction whatsoever. Once the dog calms down you should wait a few seconds get it to sit (compliance sit) and then give your dog some (calm) attention/praise. This works better for smaller dogs rather than bigger ones.

I know some behavioural practitioners are not fans of this solution but I list it as part of the overall solution mix as I know, in many cases, it does work. That being said, the preferred option would always be to get the dog to perform an action that you would like it to do instead (like 'sit'). It should also be noted that this technique does require some patience and stamina on your part because some dogs can be pretty stubborn with their insistence of getting your attention and/or interaction by jumping up and demanding it.

2. Dog to Dog/People etc Reactivity

There are a lot of reasons why dogs choose to react in certain ways to other dogs and people etc. We can never assume it is for play nor, equally, aggression. To be fair, because I have no way of knowing this, I will focus on redirection and desensitisation techniques rather than root cause. As there are a lot of similarities on how you would deal with dog reactivity whether it be over-excitement or aggression, it will not matter to much as to why your dog is reacting the way it is. If, at any point, it does I will note it down specifically. The aim of the 'reactivity' program is to pre-empt (where possible), redirect and then re-engage. As with the jumping up program, the aim here is to reduce these (emotional) 'events' to 'non-events' at worst, or even better, 'positive/energy-balanced events'. So how do we do this?

Step 1: When out walking with your dog keep a look out for any potential 'reaction' triggers (stimulus). Once you see a potential stimulus (i.e. dog/person) on the horizon then place your focus on your dog. You are looking for signs in your dog that it too has seen the stimulus.

Upon seeing the first change in its behaviour (i.e. heightened energy, stiffening of the body, staring, rear end (tail bone) erecting etc) then gently guide him/her away to a distance where it is no longer interested in the stimulus and get it to sit and look at you (see core training section "Look at Me"). It is important that we do this at the first sign of a body language change ensuring that you keep your dog under its reactivity threshold and guiding (not pulling) your dog away from the other dog/person. It is important to ensure that the 'guide away' is as smooth and calm as possible in order not to raise your dog's alertness/energy levels. If you were to pull your dog away then this will automatically heighten its energies, place it into more of an alert mentality and reduce the chances of you successfully gaining your dog's focus on you.

Step 2: Once you are able to successfully get to a point where you are sure your dog has noticed the stimulus in the distance but it does not react then you can begin to slowly reduce the distance between you and the other dog/person. It is important that you maintain your attention on your dog's body language at all times. Small steps are much better in the long run than trying to do too much too soon and getting so close your dog goes back into reactivity mode. The distance reduction should be in small increments each time in order to ensure that you keep your dog under its reactivity threshold at all times. Steady progress and little victories are better than pushing to far and having to continually restart again and again.

Step 3: When you get to a point where the stimulus is only about 20 or so feet away then start to arc around the dog/person and begin to walk in parallel if at all possible. You don't want to your dog to meet face-to-face just now as this may be viewed as confrontational by your dog or the other dog. Your dog's focus should still be on you and the reward of the redirection rather than eye contact of the other dog/person. In addition, if you can manoeuvre your dog so you are downwind of the dog/person this will allow your dog to catch the scent of the stimulus and, hopefully, associate this with the positive interaction and rewards that you are giving.

Step 4: Repeat step 3 until you are able to be almost within just a bit more than arms-length distance of the stimulus. Once you are at this stage you should have your dog looking (checking back/up) at you frequently. At this point you should be looking to pass the stimulus from the rear end, or if not possible, from side on (parallel facing). As you pass the stimulus keep rewarding your dog (praise, treats) as you go by. Again, other than using 'look at me' or 'your dog's name' then no other verbal instructions should be issued. When you do say "look at me" or your dog's name then the tone should always be fun and inviting. Once you are able to pass without your dog reacting then you just need to repeat the exposure to this until it becomes embedded.

Step 5: Once your dog is showing no negative reactivity to the stimulus then you can allow it to briefly stop and sniff the stimulus and then quickly move on (initially a 3 second meet, greet and move). You should not give any instruction and you should not engage at all with the stimulus.

Once the 3-second introduction is made then you should calmly move on and away from the stimulus. If this is successful and no negative reaction has taken place then after a few steps stop and reward your dog so he/she knows it has done well.

During such exercises, as above, you should always be looking out for signs of stress and be prepared to take the training back a few stages if you see that your dog is showing any signs of stress or discomfort. You do not want to rush progress and potentially make the situation worse by increasing your dog's negativity to the stimulus due to over exposure far too soon. There is no time limit on this and you must always progress at the pace of your dog rather than your want as this is the only way you will achieve embedded long-term positive results. Even small steps forward are better than no steps forward or any steps backward!

Step 6: For any new behaviour to become embedded it can take between 2-6 months of regular exposure. Even if your dog is 'getting it' maintain the program for a least a couple of months after 'success' to ensure that the new behaviour becomes part of its life's rules.

NOTE: Don't reward the growl. If your dog is growling or barking then, no matter where your dog's focus is (even if it is on you) do not issue any type of reward as you may be, in your dog's mind, rewarding the growl and not the fact that it's focus is on you.

IMPORTANT: If you think that your dog wants to, or thinks it needs to, inflict actual harm on a person or another dog then that is the point to call in a dog behaviour specialist, preferably one that specialises in dog aggression.

If your dog is lunging and showing a clear desire to attack (rather than just barking), or you feel that it has the real potential to follow-through and inflict a bite etc, then this is the time to get professional support as no book can give you the bespoke guidance that your dog will need. There is no way around this. You dog is crying out for help and, at this level, it does require specific (to your dog) advice rather than general advice and tips.

3. Separation Anxiety

Separation anxiety is one of the biggest causes of stress and home/furniture destruction. In the modern world it is inevitable that you have to leave your dog(s) alone some of the time and often for many hours on end. This is a big deal for your dog as they are bred to be sociable and thrive on human company. Knowing this then you will understand that you need to build up 'absence' acceptance in your dog in very small and steady steps. If you try to do too much too soon your dog will treat this program with mistrust and this will make your job significantly more challenging. To a dog both leaving the home and **<u>returning back</u>** are **BIG** events that signal cause for celebration or concern and both of which need to be managed and controlled. For best results, you need to nullify the 'event' of leaving and the 'event' of returning in equal measure.

Firstly, you need to ensure that your dog cannot predict when you are actually leaving. Therefore, you need it to experience a series of false starts. These 'false starts' are where you go through your normal leaving routing (i.e. putting your jacket on) but don't actually leave but, instead, sit back down and resume what you had been doing previously. In this type of exercise, as with other programs, it is important the you offer no interaction with your dog as you are looking for your dog to work things out and, eventually, to reduce the leaving event to a non-event.

Continue the above to the point where you can open the front door and close it again then going to sit back down to resume your previous activity with no emotional response activity from your dog. If this is going well and your dog is not increasing its stress or negative emotion then you can extend this further by opening the door and actually go out for a couple of seconds but then come back in, sit down and watch TV etc with no engagement with your dog. The aim is for your dog to get 'bored' with the comings and goings and to, basically, not really care about what you are doing.

Repeat the leaving the house exercise but slowly extend and randomise the time out (i.e. 5 secs, 10 secs, 20 secs, 5 secs etc) right up until you can stay outside for 2+ minutes. Again, at no time do you interact with your dog. As with the jumping up program, you are teaching your dog that the comings and goings that happen are perfectly natural and nothing to be concerned or excited about.

Your dog will be reassured that you always return and this is the key lesson you want your dog to learn. When you do return, there should be no drama therefore nothing for your dog to get excited about. The returning (home) element is absolutely vital to the success of this program and, if this part is not adhered to, then the whole program is at high risk of failure.

Once you are able to leave the house and stay out, with no adverse reactions, for 2-3 minutes then it will just become a matter of continued practice with varying and random durations.

Once you get to the stage where you can leave for 5 to 10 minutes with no issues then you can look to introduce something for your dog to focus on. It is often the first 10 to 20 minutes that are the most traumatic for a dog when you leave therefore, to reduce the impact of any stress that may arise in this vital period you can give your dog something to focus on. This will not only ensure that your dog is fully occupied when you leave but, hopefully, it will eventually associate you leaving to go out as the signal that something good is coming for it.

To successfully achieve this when you are ready to leave (but before you put your coat on) you can give your dog a Kong (with some paste/treats inside) or such like to chew on/play with (focus on) when you leave. It is important however, as with the leave procedure that you do this with no, or as little, fuss as possible.

So, in full view of your dog, place the Kong/toy/chew in your dog's crate (if you use a crate), dog bed or, if you don't have a crate or dog bed, then at the far end of the room you last leave from and, with no interaction with your dog, leave as normal. Assuming that you have managed to successfully complete the above program for leaving the home with no issues then your dog will not be anxious when you now leave and should be calm and curious enough to explore the 'gift' you have left. It is not that important what the actual 'gift' is but only that it is safe for your dog to have when unsupervised and that should occupy your dog for the initial 5-10 minutes, or longer, after you leave.

Doing the above will not only mentally tire your dog, but it will also relax it.

I would also suggest, if at all possible, that it would be beneficial to ensure that your dog has no access to see (or hear (directly)) out into the street, yard etc. To help combat the sounds coming from outside I would recommend putting on a radio to give some background sound and reduce the impact of any sounds that may emanate from outside. Reggae or soft rock seems to hit the spot with many dogs therefore if you can find a channel that plays this type of music predominantly then you have hit the jackpot.

4. Barking

Before we begin I do need to set out my thoughts on barking. For me, barking is not, and should not be the issue it clearly is. Dogs bark. The only ethical way I know of to 100% guarantee no barking is either not getting a dog in the first place or to get a Basenji (which is a dog breed that cannot bark but it can howl!). I don't support the extreme or punitive measures that some others promote to overcome 'problem' barking such as dogs being hit (corrected) or even being surgically operated on to remove their ability to bark, which unbelievably does happen! I, personally, think these are both cruel and very unnecessary.

Barking is important to dogs and some dogs are more vocal than others (yes, I am looking at you Mr Jack Russell Terrier). We need to remember that barking serves a purpose to both human and dogs as it warns of strangers, dangers and mangers…well, not really mangers but I just wanted to put something there that rhymed and 'mangers' came to mind. Barking can also be a very effective energy release. Unfortunately, barking can also often be a demand whereby your dog gently 'reminds' you that "I am here, I want that, play with me etc". Unfortunately, one of the top reasons for dogs being placed in shelters to be rehomed is 'problem barking'.

We, as responsible guardians, do need to control and manage barking opportunities and, of course, barking durations. In my experience, it is not barking as such that is seen as an issue but moreover uncontrolled barking. To this end, here is a few solutions to reduce the barking.

a. Don't bark!

It always amazes me that very often the first thing we do when our dog goes off on a barking frenzy is join in. When we yell at our dog to stop barking, or repeatedly issue the stop barking (i.e saying no) instruction, then it becomes a bit of an oxymoron. We are 'asking' for a behaviour to end via enacting the exact same type of behaviour ourselves. When we are yelling at our dog to stop barking our communication is riddled with emotion which, very often, heightens the dog's anxieties and energies further encouraging the barking to continue and not end. In addition, if your dog is mid-flow in the bark, do you actually think it will listen or actually hear you? Of course, a sharp vocal interrupt (like 'No' or Stop') may work but it will be inconsistent and may only work short term. Honestly, you really don't need to join in the conversation. Instead why not try one of the following: -

b. Reward the silence

For generalised 'excitement', 'exuberant' or 'demand' barking, where your dog is not barking in reaction to any particular stimulus, then we can, if you have the patience, wait it out and reward the 'breaks' in the barking. This will teach the dog that it is silence that gets the good stuff and not the noise it makes. A barking dog will naturally need to take a break when barking so, when it does, wait a second or two then issue a command such as "silence" and immediately issue it a treat.

Initially, the barking is likely to resume and when it does reward the next break in much the same fashion as above. Reward the small wins. If your dog is thinking about barking but doesn't then even that deserves a reward. The best way to correct a behaviour is often before it starts. You see, as your dog is now not automatically going into barking mode, then it is making a choice and the silence, or slight whimper, is the correct choice. Prevention is always better than cure. Just remember to use the command word (i.e. silence) when issuing the reward. You are looking for your dog to associate the command (i.e. silence) with not barking and being rewarded adequately for its refrain in barking.

After several repetitions your dog should start making the connection between the command and the reward. When you feel that this is the case then you can test this by issuing the instruction mid-bark and if your dog stops and looks for the reward then you have achieved the desired outcome. From herein it is practice, practice, test, and practice some more.

The above will work for a lot of dogs but certainly not all. This exercise will not work though if your dog is 'reactive' barking to a person or another dog. If your dog is reactive to people, or dogs, or something else then you should address the 'reason' (trigger/stimulus) for the barking rather than the barking itself (see dog to do/people reactivity program noted previously).

c. **Teach to speak**

This may seem a bit counter-intuitive but by teaching your dog to bark on cue you will also be teaching it to be silent on cue also.

The first step would be to teach your dog to bark on cue. To do this get a treat, or toy, that you know your dog will be really interested in. Let your dog see the treat/toy and keep it quite close to your dog's face but hold on to it. Your dog will try and get the item but should start getting frustrated at not being able to therefore it will no doubt let out a bark (or the start of a bark) to let you know what it wants. When this happens immediately give your dog the item/treat and take a few seconds pause. There is no instruction to be given at this stage. Repeat this until you feel that your dog has worked out that the barking gets access to the reward.

When you are at the stage where your dog will have worked out that barking gets the goods so you can now introduce a command (i.e. "speak"). Now when your dog barks, immediately say "speak" and give it the reward. Repeat this many times until you are comfortable that your dog is getting this 99% of the time. If so, keep on with the program but this time when you issue the command slightly delay the issuing of the reward.

Again, after many repetitions you can test if your dog has made the association of the commend to the required response. If so, great but if not, just keep practising. Your dog will get it, trust me.

To test the command connection make sure the toy/treat is not in view and issue your 'speak' command. If your dog responds correctly then reward it accordingly but if not, just keep on working on the command/action association. If you get to the point that your dog understand the connection and responds correctly then now you can gradually increase the time duration between getting the response and giving the reward.

Once your dog 'speaks' to command reliably then you can now turn your attention to the 'quiet' command.

To achieve this, you need to get your dog into a high state of arousal. I know, I would normally not recommend this but, for this exercise, we do need to 'generate some barking'. Once your dog is hyped enough to issue a bark then upon hearing that bark then immediately STOP all activity and issue the command (i.e. "quiet") followed immediately by issuing a reward. This time it is important that you issue the quiet command from the start in order not to undo the 'speak' achievements.

Repeat this until your dog starts to connect the quiet command with the reward. Once your dog gets to this stage, of responding correctly to the quiet command, then you can start to delay the issuing of the reward. From herein, as with all training programs, it is rinse and repeat.

When you are confident that your dog has made a solid connection to the command and how it should respond then you are ready to step it all up a gear. This time get someone else to act as the 'agitator' and let them get your dog excited. Now, whilst your dog is in this excited state, issue the 'quiet' command at a level where your dog will hear it over-and-above the noise from it (and the other person) and, if you get the required response, issue the reward. If you don't get the required response, or if it was a bit weak, then just keep on practising alone and, every now and again, in order to test the effectiveness of the command, try to initiate a response when your dog is engaged (excitedly) with someone else. It is hard but, if you persevere, you will get there.

From herein it is just practice, practice and more practice for both the speak and quiet commands.

d. Pre-emptive strike

This exercise is great for teaching your dog that it does not need to bark to in order get the good things in life. This exercise does require good timing but if you can crack it then you can basically stop a bark behaviour in its tracks.

To get started, as with the 'look at me' training you need your dog to focus on you. Assuming that your dog has managed to successfully perform the 'look at me' what you are looking for here is to reward the silence as well as the eye contact.

To start, get your dog to look at you as you would in the 'look at me' exercise. Maintain the look at me position until you see your dog become a bit fidgety and getting ready to bark. Once you see the first sign of your dog readying itself for a bark issue a reward along with the command "quiet". Repeat this over and over again each time trying to catch the bark before it happens.

Don't worry if you do not get this 100% as sometimes the bark will shoot out before you have a chance to act, especially if you have a particularly vocal dog. If this happens just ignore it and continue with the activity as if the bark had never happened.

If all goes well and your dog is getting it then still issue the command (quiet) but slightly delay the issuing of the reward. Continue the reward delay until you can issue the command and get a non-bark response for about 10 seconds or, so.

Eventually, with enough practice and good timing, you should be able to issue the command any time you see your dog getting ready to bark.

e. **Action interrupt**

The action interrupt approach is a form of interruption and (then) redirection. Here the aim is to acknowledge your dog for 'speaking' to you and thank it for doing so then redirect it onto something else. It may seem strange that we are thanking our dog for performing something that we prefer it did not. That's not really what is going on here. Dogs bark and the bark for a reason. If you acknowledge the bark then the dog will (eventually) learn that you have heard it and that it no longer needs to continue (barking). Then, using the 5 Cs, briskly walk away from your dog and simultaneously call it over to you. Once it comes over to you then get it into a compliance sit (or stay/lie down) and reward it appropriately for doing so. After you have got your dog's focus on you then guide your dog to what you would prefer it to do (even if this is a 'go rest' (see game 7)). It is important that you replace your dog's desire to bark onto something else because, should you not, your dog has got nothing else to focus on and no reason not to back to the place where the barking started.

What you are teaching your dog here is that its barking has a purpose, you have acknowledged that purpose and it gets it reward for alerting you. Then you are redirecting your dog's focus onto something else and from the stimulus that triggered the barking in the first place.

f. **Disappointing demands**

The aim of this program is to let your dog know that demands from it don't get what it is demanding to get. Therefore, if your dog is demanding (barking/pawing) for your attention then let it know you that you disapprove by creating distance from it and, if feasible, walking out of the room into another whilst, at the same time, paying no attention at all to your dog.

By doing this. you are letting your dog know two things:-

1) that you are not going to rewards its demands by engaging with it and

2) you disapprove and show this by creating distance from it.

Your dog will learn that barking will not achieve the interactions (rewards) it did previously and will learn to refrain from, or lessen, this activity.

It is important that when you do get the 'quiet' that you desire that you reward this and let him/her know that you do approve. Even if the barking does not stop altogether it should reduce significantly.

5. Mounting / Humping

This behaviour is often confused with a desire for sex from a dog. However, there are many reasons as to why some dogs display humping/mounting behaviour and many of these have nothing to do with sex. It is also a myth that only unneutered males hump/mount as this is not the case. I have seen this from neutered males as well as both spayed and unspayed female dogs.

Assuming that there is no bitch on heat that is attracting the mounting behaviour then you need to address and redirect the behaviour. To do this you must issue an action interrupt (i.e. the 'No' procedure) and then guide your dog to a more acceptable activity. If you don't offer the redirected activity then the action interrupt command is likely to be ignored or, at best, you will get a temporary interruption whereby your dog will be looking to resume the old behaviour at the earliest opportunity.

The alternative activity needs to be of equal, or greater, value to your dog than the act of humping. Humping/Mounting is a pleasurable activity and is a natural part of dog play. We, as humans, quite rightly, don't like to see this as we know what the purpose of mounting is, and this makes us feel uncomfortable. However, to a dog, or dogs, it is just play and an energy release. What it isn't is dominance or, if it is male on male or female on female, gay sex. Yes, the humper may be aroused but this is just a physical consequence of the activity itself which, at its root, is often both play or an energy release rather than anything sexual.

6. Resource guarding

A dog that tends to aggressively protect its food, toys etc is a fearful dog. It may not be generally fearful of other dogs or people but it is fearful that it will lose what it has got.

If you have a tendency to take food or toys away that your dog is interested in, possibly to show your dog that you are the 'alpha' (sic) then you will be viewed with mistrust and your dog will look to defend what it has. This is not a good situation and, by extension, your dog may extend its view of this and apply the same defence response to all people.

Remember dogs are primal and food is a vital resource. If you have a dog that does resource guard then you need to change the relationship between you and its food. You really want your dog to view you as a positive addition and not a potentially punitive one. To do this I would suggest the following: -

a. At feeding times don't give your dog its full amount straight away. Instead put a small portion of its food in and let it begin. Whilst it is eating, introduce into its bowl some more food. However, if your dog is suspicious and is looking to negatively react to your action then, initially, you may have to introduce the second amount via a second bowl and slide it in. Thereafter, continue to introduce its food bit by bit until it has finished its meal amount.

The fact the you are giving your dog food and not taking its food will, through time, teach your dog that you coming over is a good thing as it can mean that more food is coming.

b. Again, at feeding times, get your dog to sit and wait before you put its bowl down. This will, again, remind your dog that you are the provider of good things and to get such things it needs to pay attention to you.

c. Why not make a game of meal times and, if using dry food, you can scatter feed the food for your dog to hunt out. If you use wet food then hide the bowl out of sight and let your dog hunt it out. This exercise turns meal times into fun game time and, as you are the provider of the game, then your dog will associate you with the good things. It is recommended though, that you do get your dog to sit and wait before being 'released' to go find the food.

Note: If your dog is protective of a toy then introduce a toy and let it play with it. After a short period introduce a new toy and let it play with that and discreetly remove the original toy when it is fully engaged with the new toy. Do likewise with a third toy and then, after a while, go back and reintroduce the first toy again and start the program over.

IMPORTANT NOTE: Only remove a food or toy if your dog has finished the food or lost interest in the toy (possibly by walking away). One of the main issues for resource guarding in dogs is having the thing it craves. Or actively engaged with, being taken away right smack in the middle of it enjoying it. If you relate this to you how happy would you be if you were sitting down to a meal and in the middle of this someone stepped up and took it away from you. You would not be happy if this happened and, of course, it is totally understandable that your dog will not be either.

7. **Mouthing / Nipping / Mouth grabs**

This may sound super obvious but the key to stopping this unwanted behaviour is not to let it happen in the first place. Prevention, especially when it comes to this aspect, if definitely better than cure.

For example, if you have a puppy then don't accept it exploring you, or your family, with its mouth. It is natural for dogs to explore with their mouths and it is important that we allow it to do so. However, there should be a few red lines and touching skin or chewing furniture should be a just a couple of them. Given this, don't allow your puppy's teeth contact skin right from the off. A puppy is keen to learn and will quickly understand what is allowed and what is not allowed. The 'no' procedure should suffice in most puppy cases.

If you have an older dog or a particularly determined puppy then you need to up the ante somewhat. For these type of dogs you need to let them know directly that what they are doing is not acceptable whilst simultaneously removing all interaction with them. To achieve this, as soon as teeth touch skin, no matter how gently, you should let out a brief squeal or a sharp shriek (action interrupt) and immediately stop the interaction, get up and walk away. Don't speak to, or interact, while you are walking away. You want your dog to work out what has just happened. This will let your dog know that it has crossed the line and that you do not approve. After about 20-30 seconds you can resume the play but repeat the process if teeth touch skin again.

If, in the cases where your puppy or dog likes to bite and grab onto the bottom of your trousers etc, then use the 'no procedure' and stand absolutely still giving your dog no interaction whatsoever. If you just say no and then lift, or push, your dog away then you are still rewarding it with interaction therefore potentially reinforcing the behaviour that you are looking to stop. If your dog is getting no reaction from you, which is no fun for your dog, it should cease the activity. If this does not work then you may want to use the 'chewing/destruction' technique noted below.

8. Chewing / Destruction

This is a bit of a variation on the stop mouthing/biting procedure whereby you still need to interrupt the activity but this time you need to introduce something else to do or, better still, something else to chew on. Dogs not only like to chew, they need to chew, especially teething puppies. This is a natural activity and is good for maintaining strength and cleanliness of their teeth. I would never recommend removing all chewing opportunities but, instead, providing acceptable chewing outlets. Chewing also gets the mental juices flowing so it is great mental stimulation for a dog also.

If your dog persists in chewing on what you would like them not to chew on such as furniture, then you need to either change what the alternative is that is on offer or make the act of 'not chewing' more appealing. Changing what is on offer is quite straight forward and it may be trial and error in finding that one thing that satisfies you and your dog. For my 2 dogs I use naturally sourced deer antlers but there are plenty of artificial items out there that can more than satisfy the dog's need in this respect.

If you need to 'incentivise' your dog toward the item of your choice then you can smear it with peanut butter (choose a brand that has no xylitol in it as this chemical is very bad for dogs) or squeezy cheese etc. Moreover, as an alternative to chewing, if you are able to pack a Kong type item with small treats that will take your dog time to tease out, then all the better.

9. **Stealing Food / Begging / Counter surfing**

A dog begging at the table whilst you eat is often off putting and, quite frankly, a bit rude. As you are the resource provider, and should be accepted as such, then you should also be able to leave food on the table without running the risk of your dog taking it.

To counter 'begging' behaviour you will need to redirect this activity. To this end, I would recommend you do so via the 'go rest' exercise. It is also a good idea, if at all possible, and if you tend to eat at the same time each night, for your dog to have its main meal at the same time as you. However, if you tend not to eat at the same time each night then I would just focus on the 'go rest' training.

To stop your dog doings things like counter surfing then you will need to train your dog to leave 'temptations' it may see alone and, of course, be adequately rewarded for doing so. Ideally, you would want to dog proof the area and remove temptation in the first place but I understand that this is not always feasible or practical. Given this, I have noted below the steps you can take to train your dog to abstain for food theft.

Step 1: Place a tempting plate of food on top of a table. Make sure your dog can see, and smell, this.

Step 2: Sit your dog quite near this table and, using a high value treat/reward, get your dog to focus on you (i.e. via "look at me" exercise) and reward it each time it looks at you.

Step 3: Once your dog is looking at you in expectation of getting a reward from you then we can up the 'temptation' by pointing to the plate, then obtaining the direct eye contact from your dog and, of course, issuing the reward when it does so.

Step 4: Using the 5 Cs repeat step 3 but issue the command "leave it" and, again, obtain and reward eye contact from your dog.

Step 5: Move the plate a bit closer to the edge of the table and repeat step 4.

Step 6: Again, move the plate further towards the edge of the table and keep doing this until it is impractical to move the plate further without it falling.

Step 7: Now move the plate to the floor and, if all goes well, next to you. If your dog moves forward when you are moving the plate then return it to the table and wait a few seconds and try again.

Each time your dog moves forward to try and investigate the plate then return it back to the table. Once you get to be able to place the plate on the floor and successfully issue the "leave it" command and get full compliance then you can move onto step 8.

Step 8: If your dog is showing no sign of trying to get to the plate then take a step back, issue the "leave it" command, and, assuming no movement from you dog, step back and reward your dog.

Step 9: Repeat step 8 but increase your distance from the your dog and the plate a step at a time (always ensuring that your dog is not looking to move, or lunge, toward the plate). If it does try to get the plate then just go back a few steps and rebuild. Remember to take regular breaks from this exercise.

Step 10: Hopefully you can now get to, or very near, the door. At this point, issue the instruction, leave the room (but still staying in sight of your dog), wait a second or two, then return and reward your dog if it has not moved.

Step 11: Repeat step 10 but this time stay out of sight and slightly increase the duration before your return to and, of course, reward your dog if it has not moved. At this point the aim is to increase the out of sight duration a few seconds at a time until you can stay out of sight for circa 30 seconds with no mishaps.

Step 12: If you get to this point and you can stay out of sight for about 30 seconds then start placing the temptation in different places in the room, issue the instruction, leave, wait then return. From herein it is just practice, practice and more practice.

10. Chasing / Herding objects

If your dog has originally been bred to herd then it very likely that it will have a propensity to chase and herd. If your dog is not allowed to chase/herd then it will need to be allowed an alternative that gives it a reward almost equal to what chasing/herding would have given it.

Collies and other herding dogs in general tend to be highly intelligent dogs that require a lot of mental stimulation.

Game playing is a good way to satisfy your dog's need to 'herd'. These need not be herding games as such but they do need to be both mentally taxing and high energy. I have noted below some suggestions in this respect: -

    a. **Playing fetch**: A good 10 - 15 minute game of fetch, with a ball or a frisbee, is a fantastic game for all dogs but especially Collies etc.

b. **Agility**: Agility is a great outlet for these types of dogs as it requires a lot of discipline and focus as well as being a great physical outlet.

c. **Flyball**: As with agility this activity will test your dog both mentally and physically.

d. **Treibball**: This is a relatively new activity that I do not profess to know much about. It has been coined, by some, as soccer for dogs. The aim of the game is to work in conjunction with other dogs to move and manipulate large inflated balls across a field and into a goal. As you can appreciate this will really give your dog a solid physical and mental workout.

e. **Fetch by name**: This is an extension of the 'choose a toy' game whereby not only will your dog pick out the named toy but it will also bring it back to you. Assuming your dog is able to play the choose a toy competently and reliably then all you need to do is introduce the 'bring' element of this game.

To do this when your dog selects the correct toy then hold off issuing the reward marker or the reward until it actually picks the toy up. At this point call your dog over whilst taking a step back. If your dog comes over to you still carrying the toy then mark and reward it. If it drops the toy then just restart and rebuild.

Once your dog is regularly bringing over the correct toy then gradually increase your distance from the toy and mark and reward when your dog brings the toy to you. This will all take a bit of time but it is a great game for you and your dog and a great game to show off to friends and family.

f. **Hide and seek**: Using the sit/stay command have your dog wait whilst you go and hide. Initially hide in plain sight and, assuming your dog is still in its original (starting) position then call it over and mark and reward it for doing so. You only need to hide in plain sight until your dog figures out what it is to do in this game. Gradually increase the distance and then step it up by hiding out of sight before you call your dog over.

g. **Give your dog a job**: Why not get a back pack and place some water bottles, poo bags etc in it and give your dog a job when out on walks?

Even the act of just carrying an object for you is often a good mental release for some dogs.

Note: please don't over-burden your dog by placing a back-pack, or placing items in the back-pack, that will prove strenuous for your dog to carry. This is especially important if your dog is under 12 months old as its bones are still growing.

11. Obsessive compulsive behaviour

Behaviours that don't seem to serve an obvious purpose and are continually being repeated are often born from an obsessive compulsive disorder (OCD) in your dog. An OCD is a coping behaviour that, to your dog, is self-rewarding but can become habituated if allowed to be repeated over time. Examples of this would be light or shadow chasing, window or floor licking, licking own fur or paws etc.

If left unaddressed then this behaviour could cause both physical and/or health issues. It is not uncommon for vets to attend to a dog has licked its fur away and its skin red raw.

Although it may not always be possible, if you can identify the root cause of this behaviour then it will make it easier to resolve, as you can deal with the cause and not just the symptom. If not, then you will need to generalise the behaviour itself but should still be able to stop, or at least reduce, the occurrences of it.

In my experience, very often, OCD behaviour is a result of not enough mental stimulation. Your dog may feel it is in a mental prison and seek to pass the time and entertain itself by performing this repetitive behaviour and through time this behaviour becomes addictive and compulsive. In some other dogs it may be an outlet for an unsatisfied breed predisposition. Light, shadow or fly chasing tend to be born of breed behaviour deficiencies.

Assuming that both mental and breed requirements are being satisfied then the crucial element to stop/reduce OCD behaviours is to interrupt and redirect it. You do this by: -

a. Interrupt the activity with an 'action interrupt' sound. This is a short sharp sound that will cut through the dogs focus on the activity and onto the origin of the noise, you.

b. Call your dog over to you whilst creating distance from where the activity was taking place.

c. Get your dog to give you a compliance sit (or lie down) and reward this.

d. Go play a game with your dog or give it
    something else to do that it can focus on for a
    least a minute or two (chew toy etc).

e. If you can, close off or restrict access to the area
    where such activity is likely to take place.

f. Repeat all of the above until your dog's
    compulsion to perform this activity is reduced
    (which it will do naturally over time if unable to
    perform it without being interrupted and stopped).

    If the redirected activity is of equal, or greater,
    value than the value your think it received from
    the OCD activity itself then the extinction of the
    OCD behaviour will be quicker. If not, then it
    will take longer and sometimes a lot longer. In
    either circumstance it will take over 3 months of
    continued 'OCD interrupt and redirect'
    application before your dog starts to unlearn this
    behaviour.

12. Attention addiction

I have added this 'issue' as more of a reminder note than
anything else. I have found, in my years of dog training and
behavioural modification that, amongst the circumstantial

influences that affect behaviour there are a couple of commonalities that seem to be a factor more often than not.

Energy is one, and this is well addressed in this book. Confidence is another which, again, I have addressed elsewhere. However, attention addiction is another.

What I mean by this is that a dog may feel that it needs you, or someone else, to be around and, often, make decisions for it. Your dog may feel it does not have the skills or confidence to do so by itself. The problem, if this is the case, is that your dog will not own any positive rewards it may achieve as it will not recognise these have arisen because of choices it has made. This means that you will be consigned to leading and directing your dog for all, if not most, of its life. This is not an ideal situation as you want your dog to learn from the choices it makes and grow in confidence and contentment from doing so.

I very often find that attention addiction can arise from guardians who tend to talk to their dog too much, interact too often and protect too much (or too soon) thus stifling experience and decision making in your dog. This will lead to inhibiting your dog from enjoying and being comfortable in its own space. The latter point of space is important as dogs need time to relax and reflect as part of their learning and development process.

If you make your dog the centre of your world then it will become used to being the centre of your world, see no reason to make its own decisions and will come to expect this day in day out, thus, become addicted. This will make times when you cannot give your dog the same level of attention very difficult for you and for your dog as neither of you have adequately prepared for it. In addition, this will also blur the lines of you being the resource provider and security giver as your constant interaction will haze out the rules and, because of this, your dog will internalise its own 'helplessness' and will know that it can rely on you to get what it wants (think primal).

Given this, I would always advise allowing 'down time' for both you and your dog as well as talking with purpose rather than comfort, especially in core training time. There is always room for comfort chat and that is never to be discouraged but if this comes at the cost of inhibiting your dog's ability to make decisions and be comfortable without you being around then than is a bit of a problem. If you can limit comfort chat to down time then this will greatly support your dog's self-confidence and reduce the risk of any over-reliance on you from arising in the first place.

Post-Traumatic Stress Disorder (PTSD)

I have left this section until the end as it so important and so often misunderstood. PTSD can negatively affect every element of dog training, behaviour modification and even general dog guardianship. Yes, as with humans, dogs can suffer PTSD too. That being said, there should be a clear distinction made between a dog that is generally nervous or negative in character to one that has become so due to some incident in its past. There are a lot of similarities in how you would deal with a dog that is, in general, overly-pessimistic, cautious and fearful to one that suffers from PTSD but there are a few significant differences.

So how do you tell the difference between a dog that is suffering from PTSD to one that is generally fearful and negative? The short answer is if the behaviour has always been there and is, in your view, just the way your dog is then this is part of its natural character. If, however, your dog produces a sudden change in behaviour, i.e. suddenly becoming fearful or withdrawn, and this continues over time, with no sign of abating, then this could be PTSD. I do accept that I am over-simplifying this but I have just noted the above for the purposes of basic understanding in order to try and plan effectively on how to help your dog overcome its fear.

I also accept that your dog may have suffered an incident when it is with its litter-mates that you have no idea about or that 'something may have happened' that, again, you have no idea about and could not identify. Finally, I also accept that not all dogs will be able to overcome their PTSD, or, in some cases, their generalised fear, and the dog, and the environment etc, will have to be managed and controlled for the rest of its life. Thankfully, although far from unknown, these situations are not very common and certainly does not mean that a 'fearful' dog cannot live a fulfilling life because this is not the case, it will just need to be carefully managed.

So how do you help your dog overcome its 'fear'? The secret to overcoming fear is actually no secret you just need to help your dog feel better about the world around it. Simples. If only.

Firstly, helping your dog overcome fear takes time, lots of time. Time from you in training and time for your dog to readjust to the new way of seeing and doing things. There is no way around this, no quick fix and definitely no short cuts. If your dog is generally nervous, fearful or fear reactive and you think you can 'fix' this in 3-4 months then I am going to be the bearer of bad news. Changing a nervous dog to a more confident dog takes many months, possibly years and, on occasion, a lifetime. Your dog is scared and we are trying to convince it not to be scared and, hopefully, be happy and confident instead. Not an easy task especially if your dog was born fearful or became (embedded) fearful at a very young age, i.e. via the imprinting period or its 'fear' stage. No, changing your dog's demeanour is going to take time, lots of time, and patience, lot's of patience.

Dog trainers and behaviourists will, in cases where the 'fear' is related to a stimulus such as dogs or people will put together programs of desensitisation, counter conditioning and, for some old school practitioners, immersion therapies. For PTSD and/or stimulus responses these can, and often do, work well and I have noted some of these in this section but, again, these will take time. For generalised fear though, where your dog is seemingly fearful of everything and usually very 'skittish' or has got a very profound 'startle-response' (where it seems to jump at even the smallest sound or movement), then you have nothing definitive to refer to when trying to counter-condition, desensitise of 'immerse'. Just for super-clarity I do not condone immersion therapy but I have to mention it as it is one of the techniques that do get used by some dog professionals. In such cases you need to rebuild from the inside out.

What I mean by 'building from the inside out' is that you need to get back to the core of the actions/responses your dog 'feels' it needs to give in order navigate the world around it in order to keep itself safe and satisfied. I have noted previously in this book that dogs are primal in their thinking and operate within its survival resonance where emotion is the key driver to their actions. Dogs wear their hearts on their sleeves and the don't do subtle. If they like it then you will know it and, conversely, the same is true if they don't. The 'what's in it for me' (WIIFM) principle rules the psychological roost as it were and that there lies the problem.

You see, and this is true of most training, you try and elicit positive behaviours via the reward of 'good things' when it does well, which you know will appeal to your dog's WIIFM. But how can you breakthrough this emotional barrier when 'everything' around your dog is the issue? This is where you need your dog to take 'decision ownership'.

Decision ownership is where your dog has taken time to solve a problem and when it has done so successfully is adequately rewarded for its efforts. You need to exercise and satisfy your dog's mental capacity. You do this through play. Not just any play though, but through 'brain games'.

All good training sessions are preceded by exercise and games in order to expel any excess energy your dog may have. This will allow your dog to be able to focus on you and your guidance without the need to run around like a loon in order to burn off energy. However, for building confidence, you need to introduce your dog to 'brain games' where it needs to use its 'grey matter' in order to solve a puzzle, or task, in order to access the reward. If your dog is engaged in a brain game then it will be focused on the task in hand and not the surrounds. I have noted below a small selection of brain game suggestions that you could try: -

A. **Puzzle games**: There are lots of these on the market and can easily be purchased online or from a Pet Store. I would note though that puzzle games are a bit Marmite for dogs, they either love them or just plain not interested in them. As with anything it will be trial and error but don't worry if this is not for your dog as there are plenty of alternatives. Anther word of caution is that if the game has small (breakable) parts or your dog is particularly destructive then I would not recommend this option.

B. **Go Hunt**: If your dog likes to play with a ball, or a favourite toy, then why not hide it in different places and allow your dog to search for it? Initially start hiding close by, in full view of your dog, then slowly hide out of sight and extend the distance of the placement away from your dog.

C. **Snuffle Mat**: A snuffle mat is a rubber-based mat with holes throughout. You attach strands of cloth/fleece through these holes covering the full surface area of the mat. After you have put together your snuffle mat (the effect you are going for is for the surface to look like a deep pile rug). The aim is then to hide little treats within the cloth and then let your dog search them out.

D. **Scatter Feed**: This is a great game for dogs who are dry food fed. Why not ditch the bowl and scatter you dog's food and allow it to hunt it out?

E. **Treats in a Plastic Bottle**: Using an empty and cleaned out plastic fizzy drink bottle drop a treat, or treats within the bottle and let your dog work out how to access the treat(s). Note: don't replace the cap/lid on the bottle. Also, to ensure that your dog does not swallow any shards of the plastic does not become ragged and sharp, you will need to ensure that your dog is fully monitored during this activity.

F. **Kong Play**: Using a Kong, or similar, pack the toy with dog friendly peanut butter, or mushed up kibble, and pack it into the gap. Give this to your dog for it to work out how to get out all of the goodness you have packed inside. This activity mimics dog's trying to get marrow from a bone.

If you play brain games in different places outside then this will also show your dog that play is not confined to home and that everywhere that you both go is a 'potential' play spot. This will teach your dog three things. 1) Outside, or new places, are not to be viewed as a potential threat but, instead, a potential games spot. 2) When your dog achieves success and accesses the reward(s) then this will also release serotonin (feel good chemical) whilst it is in-situ in the (once) 'scary' place and, via continued repetition, will becomes desensitized to any negative perceptions of the area. 3) This is the key take way. Your dog will receive a positive outcome (the reward) from the decisions (working out) it made and, because of this, will begin to learn to have more confidence in its own decisions going forward. Point 3 underpins everything and is the key building block to your dog viewing the world in a more positive light, having more confidence in its decision making and, crucially, owning the decisions it made. Everything thereafter is just continued exposure to mental workouts, in different places, at different times, with, if possible, different people around.

For more pessimist dogs, that ones that tend to give up quickly or don't even have the optimism to start will require quite a bit of coaxing and support throughout but when they do starts to see the rewards for their labour then they will soon become more eager to start and continue with the mental challenges posed.

Before I move onto the section dealing with context, I would like to note at this point that sometimes a behaviour will get worse before it gets better. Some dogs are particularly resistant to change and will be more reluctant to accept the reason for change. Some dogs just don't like being told what to do or do something that they are not particularly in the mood for at the time. Such dogs may heighten the 'negative' (unwanted) behaviour or throw in a barrel load of other unwanted behaviours in order to try and get you to give in and change tact. This is called an 'extinction burst' and, much alike breaking a horse, is very much the last throw of the dice for your dog in trying to retain its previous behaviour. Nobody welcomes change and, given the rigid primal rules that dogs live by, they can be particularly resistant to change. Consistency and persistence is the key here to overcoming such resistance.

Context is Everything

A factor that is often overlooked when dealing with dog behaviour is context. As stated previously in the book, everything has a survival value to a dog and these survival values are directly aligned to the environment or context in which the 'value item' resides. Given this, dogs will give everyone, everything and everywhere a set of contextual behavioural rules and values which will align with the dog's perceptions of how it should act in the environment it finds itself in (survival resonance).

An example of this would be that your dog may be well behaved in your home but become less well behaved when in another home such as a friend or relative's home. It is the same dog, in a similar type of environment, but acting seemingly out-of-character whilst in the other home. The reason for this is that your dog has not been taught what is, and is not, acceptable in this new (alien) environment and may also be unsure of the possible threats or rewards to be had and will be acting in accordance with its survival values.

The same principle is true also on how it sees people in interacts with. Your dog may act one way with you but in a different way with someone else. In fact, this is very common and is why everyone involved with your dog all need to be singing from the same hymn sheet and be consistent with the rules and the delivery of the rules.

Although dogs do think on a primal level this does not mean they are not intelligent as this could not be further from the truth. Added to this dogs tend to have excellent memories and are more than capable of creating (or understanding) different rules from different people and/or environments. As I had already stated, what I mean by this is that a dog may act in one way with you but in a completely different way with someone else, even if you, your dog and the 'someone else' are all together at the time.

I have lost count of the number of times I have been told a dog "responds to him/her but not me...". If I can go back to 'Dools Rules' which I had cited at the start of this book you will note that we, as people, act likewise and are very environmentally aware. The kids in the football team did not suddenly become more compliant and less troublesome in the wider community just because they were like that with Mr Dool. No, they understood what was allowed and tolerated within the team and acted accordingly. They applied context to their behaviour and decision making. Dogs are very much the same but on a more primal level and with a seemingly sixth sense!

Character and temperament aside, dogs generally do have a blank canvas to new places and people, unless they are within a fear stage of their development of course, or have had some past trauma experience in a similar environment or situation.

Therefore, given this, they will naturally explore and learn, very quickly, what rewards and dangers are to be had and they will bank this information and act accordingly.

It is very, very important, that your dog is introduced to new situations, people and places in a calm and controlled manner with you controlling access whilst giving regular feedback to your dog on what you like, and what you don't like, in respect of its behaviour. If you are consistent in this then your dog will learn to look to you for your guidance as default rather than rely on their own exploration and interpretation endeavours.

Dog Aggression

Before I commence this element, I would like to state that the following can only be a generalised overview of aggression in dogs as the causes and solutions for such are often complex and I would always recommend a dog professional that has a particular expertise in dealing with aggression issues. The key criteria when dealing with a dog that is aggressive, or shows signs of aggression, is safety. This safety extends to other dogs, other people, you and, of course, your dog.

This may sound a bit strange but aggression is not just aggression. It may not be obvious, but it is the type of aggression that will, along with the dog's physical health, history, environment and breed tendencies (if prevalent) that will need to be understood in order to provide solutions that have a real chance of success. To this end, I have listed below the 12 types of aggression I am aware of: -

1. **Fear/Nervous/Defence Aggression**

   This is the most common form of aggression in dogs. Aggression is the last line of defence after all warnings have went unheeded and the dog feels that, because it is unable to escape or avoid potential conflict or scary situation, it needs to be aggressive or actually attack.

   The key here is to, if possible, remain calm and give the dog time and space to work things out. The dog needs to have its confidence built, or rebuilt, with whatever it is that it feels is placing it under threat.

   Programs, such as the 'dog reactivity' program is one solution that can be applied. The key is all about changing the relationship and dog's perception of what it is fearful about. It may be the case that a dog will never fully get over its fear and stay within a cautious mode but as long as it can do so without feeling it needs to go into aggression/attack stance then it just becomes all about control and management. The important factor is to keep you, your dog and other dogs/people safe and this should be the number one priority in any training program you, and your dog, undergoes.

If you can, then try not to expose your dog to the stimulus that triggers its fear, especially in the short term, then work on building up its confidence in these situations.

For dogs that do suffer from reactive (fear) responses it is important that you do not focus on the stimulus of the fear to your dog but instead try to focus on having fun in the vicinity of the stimulus (but far away enough for it to notice, but not be concerned by, it). Through time, your dog will see that as you are not perturbed by the (perceived) 'threat' and that you are happy to play and have fun in such situations it will learn to take its lead from you and start to relax. It is a slow process but a worthwhile one.

As part of the confidence building process tools such as Adaptil© collars and diffusers, which mimics the release of a naturally appeasing pheromone chemical mirrors the smell of a nursing mother, may help with the confidence building process.

2. Resource Aggression

As noted in the resource guarding section the key here is to teach your dog that your presence does not mean that its food or toy is placed at risk of being taken away.

3. Confidence Aggression

This is often called 'dominance' aggression but I prefer the term confidence aggression even though, in real terms, there is really nothing to differentiate either. The reason I do not use the 'dominance' tag is that the understanding of dominance has been misunderstood, abused and used as an excuse for bullying and mistreating dogs. The prevalence of the dominance tag also lends itself to breed specific stereotyping and, in some cases, dog control legislation, which I think totally misses the point when it comes to identifying and controlling dangerous dogs and just does not work.

The solution to controlling an over-confident dog is to give it plenty of training and play, all led by you. This teaches it that you are the provider of all things good therefore it does not need to seek self-satisfaction elsewhere.

For times when your dog is playing with other dogs and becomes overly-bullish and exuberant then it is up to you to stop the game and redirect your dog's focus and energy into a lower energy activity with you. Once your dog has had time to bring its energies back down it can be allowed back to play (on a lead or long line preferably) with you watching for signs of bullying or over exuberance arising again and stopping this behaviour before it escalates. However, when stopping play it is important that you offer an alternative activity else your dog is not going to appreciate the interruption and it will, if this is the case, look to do everything it can to avoid being interrupted in the future.

4. Frustration (or Redirection) Aggression

This is where we have pushed our dog's tolerance for waiting beyond its ability to wait or we are trying to restrict or stop it from doing something it clearly wants to do.

Prevention and pre-emption is the key here with the focus on avoiding this 'frustration' from arising in the first place. If you know that your dog is likely to get to an energy point where it will be so focused on satisfying its desire that it will take unkindly to anything, or anyone, that gets in the way then you need to make sure it never gets to that stage. To this end, you need to ensure that you closely monitor your dog's energy levels and never allow it to get over aroused or over stimulated. Teaching impulse control is a great activity for teaching a dog patience and restraint. Prevention is definitely better than cure here.

5. Misdirected Aggression

This is more of an energy outburst rather than aggression per se. As with the frustration aggression it is important that you do not allow your dog to get into a high state of arousal or over-stimulation in the first place.

6. Startle (Reactive) Aggression

This is reaction is often born out of lack of confidence in a dog. If a dog is startled and this results in an aggressive response then your dog is telling you that it is unsure of what to do and, due to the lack of confidence, lashes out as its default response. You need to let your dog know that you have got its back and everything is in hand. You will want your dog to look to you for guidance when it is frightened or unsure rather than going straight to action. Plenty of games, interaction and 5 Cs communication will help here.

7. Energy Aggression

This aggression is the easiest to predict as it builds up. It may build up quickly but it does build up and if you can spot it then you can sort it. Over Stimulated play will show itself in the dog's vocal pitch getting sharper and higher and its movements becoming more frantic. If you hear a the pitch during your dog's play getting increasingly louder and sharper then interrupt it and redirect it to a more energy controlled activity (with you) until its energies reduce again. In most cases, a small time out will suffice.

Some dogs shake their head (left and right) vigorously after high energy play in order to release the built up energy. This is called a 'reset-shake'. If/when your dog has performed a 'reset shake' it should be ready to re-join the fun. If your dog regularly gets too excited then impulse control training coupled with 'low and slow' interactions will teach it to have the same level of satisfaction without the high level of energy output.

8. Anticipated Aggression

This is aggression that is born from you. What I mean by this is that your dog may pick up 'alert' signals from you, very often that you are not even aware of, and place itself in a high state of readiness for the 'anticipated' forthcoming danger.

This often arises when, because of the previous negative incidents you have had with your dog and other dogs (or people) and you spot potential trouble ahead and now go into alert mode and, almost subliminally. You tighten the lead, take deeper breaths, possibly try too hard to assure your dog (possibly with your voice breaking) that everything is okay all while releasing adrenalin (which your dog can smell) and, before you know it, you have sounded the alarm to your dog. Due to this 'signal' it will now pan and scan the environment and will no doubt find and fix its gaze on what you had already spotted.

To resolve this, and I do accept this is not easy, is to keep yourself loose and calm in this situation. You may have to fake it until you make it but your leadership is the guiding principle in how your dog reacts. Using the 5 Cs calmly guide your dog away if you can, or get its focus on you and a compliance sit until the stimulus is away (or passed), if you cannot.

9. Trained Aggression

This almost requires no explanation. Some dogs are trained for aggression. This is usually restricted to the Police or armed forces but some security companies also train their dog for aggression also. In most cases there is nothing to fear here as this is highly-trained controlled aggression with the guardians in full control of their dog. The problem lies where dogs have been training for fox hunting, hare coursing, badger baiting, pit fighting etc and, via learned experience, these dogs learn to enjoy the conflict.

Thankfully, it will be rare that you will ever come across one of these dogs but the signs to look for is a dog, or dogs, that stare and track you, or your dog, and seems to pay no heed to their guardian or anything else other than what it is focused on. These dogs may not lunge, strain or growl or bark, remember they have been trained to fight not chase away therefore making noise does not satisfy that ambition, so do not wait until you hear vocalisation. If you are in any doubt at all, about any dog, or any situation, then trust your instincts and go elsewhere. I would rather be wrong about a dog and leave than to take a chance, stay and become embroiled in 'conflict'.

If we look at things from a human perspective I am sure there have been times where you have decided to change a route when going somewhere, even if you have been down that route a million times, just because you felt uneasy. You trusted your instincts then and there is no reason to change this stance now. This way the only casualty is a bit of extra wear on our shoe leather and not a trip to the vet!

10. Sexual Aggression

Un-neutered male dogs want to mate. Un-neutered female dogs in season will want to be mated with. If a male comes across a bitch on heat it will want to 'get it on' with it and little you can do will deter it from this intention. The bitch will be a willing victim. Now, if you add another un-neutered male into the mix then you are going to have a fight. This is hormone led activity and your dog will be compelled by these hormones to act. Apart from neutering your dog and maintaining space from bitches on heat then there is not a lot else to be done here. It is basically control and management keeping your dog out of these situations.

11. Predatory Aggression

This is another common cause of aggression incidents. These usually arise when two dogs have been playing and then suddenly world war 3 breaks out. Then you look at the two dogs involved and you will see that one dog was a

Greyhound and the other dog was a Chihuahua that decided, in its wisdom, to make a fast break away. The Greyhound then went into full 'hare chase' mode and the Chihuahua, which is a ratter by breed and fearless, reacted with aggression.

As stated in the play chapter of this book. If your dog is displaying any of its breed characteristics then find a way for these to be exercised else your dog will look for a way to satisfy these desires itself and this could be, in worst case scenarios, disastrous.

12. Health/Pain/Psychological Aggression

Most, but not all, dogs are fantastic at masking pain. Showing pain is showing weakness and, going back to primal thinking, showing no pain is a survival mechanism. If your dog suddenly changes behaviour and you cannot think of an obvious reason as to why then I would always recommend a vet check-over as dogs don't change behaviour without a reason to do so. Note: A change of behaviour is always a point of note but not always a point of concern.

In addition, if we have got a dog, that, for whatever reason, did not spend the first 8 weeks of its life with its mother and siblings then it may not have experienced good social forming within this vital 'imprinting' period. If this is the case, then its brain would not have formed fully and it may struggle with social activities and interactions thereafter. If this is the case for your dog then you should control and manage exposure to other dogs and situations. This will ensure that you do not add trauma to poor development by placing your dog in a situation it clearly does not know how to deal with.

As a final note on aggression, I have stated in this book that confidence is one of the key underlying causes of behavioural issues. This is also often true of aggression in dogs. An over-confident, and often socially naïve, dog will not only ride rough-shod (bully) over some other dogs but will tend to enjoy doing so. This is not a dominant dog but a poorly trained dog that, in all likelihood, has suffered from deprived early development experiences. There are no hierarchies in place and this type of dog is not looking to be the leader of the pack but, instead, is just a demanding dog with no restraint. Conversely, if your dog is low in confidence, fearful by default and relatively timid in character then it is likely to attract bullying dogs.

I believe dogs, as do people, can develop the 'victim complex' whereby they become a constant target for thuggish and ill-mannered dogs. The key to combatting this is building the confidence in such dogs by talking less, playing lots of games and by exposing them to new experiences gradually and in a fun manner. You will note that I have said talking less and I have said this because we want our dog to work things out itself and dialogue from a person, almost irrespective of what that dialogue is, may reduce the incentive to work things out and continually look to you to provide all of the answers. A dog needs to make its own choices to enjoy the rewards of such and, as a result, grow in confidence.

'COMMON ISSUES AND CHALLENGING BEHAVIOUR' CHAPTER SUMMARY

- Right and wrong behaviour
- Bad dog 'myth'
- PERFECT Foundation
- Reflect and review
- Learn to earn
- Control and management
- Talk with purpose
- Jumping up /demanding attention
- Dog to dog/people reactivity
- Separation anxiety
- Barking
- Mouthing / Humping
- Resource guarding
- Mouthing / nipping / mouth grabs
- Chewing / destruction
- Stealing food/ / begging / counter surfing
- Chasing / herding objects
- Obsessive compulsive behaviour
- Attention addiction
- PTSD
- Context is everything
- Dog aggression

Chapter 7: Managing Set Backs

One of the main reasons for training failure is how we deal with set-backs. For the purposes of this chapter, I would include dog intransigence as a set-back. When things are not going as we would hope it is hard not to feel frustrated. It is not uncommon to think the training isn't working but, in my experience, this is rarely is this the case.

Firstly, if your dog sees an opportunity to exploit a situation for any gain it thinks it's going to get then, chances are, it will take it. So, to avoid this arising, you need to control the 'training area' as best you can to ensure that there are no 'outside' influences that are going to tempt your dog. You should also no be asking too much too soon of your dog. Dogs learn at different rates and you may need to be patient no matter how frustrating it may seem. Further, keep the sessions short and fun. By adopting all of this you will well be on your way to be set up for success and not failure but, even by doing all this, things are never guaranteed.

As with people, sometimes the training methods we deploy just don't tick the right boxes and we just don't get engagement. As I have said already, dogs are as different and as unique as we are and if your student does not learn in the way you teach then you need to try and teach in the way it learns. If this is the case then it is not a reflection on you or the training itself but it just means that your approach or incentives may need a review.

As an NLP (Neuro Linguistic Practitioner) trained communicator I know that there are many ways of communicating with people. These communication reception (learning) styles are called 'modalities' and relate to our five key senses of seeing, hearing, touch, taste and smell. What this means is that some people are emotionally predisposed to receive 'auditory' communication, as a default, where sound is more important than the visual whilst the predominantly 'visual' modality person prefers imagery, the 'kinesthetic' person prefers 'touch' related sounds and phrases whilst the 'olfactory' is more attuned to sounds relating to smell and a 'gustatory' person leans towards taste. In addition, there are also 'auditory digital' people and these type of people are more analytical and tend to focus more on procedures and sequences.

What all this means is, if we want to talk to people using language that mirrors the emotion and learning styles of the person we are communicating to then we need to understand what modality best reflects them. In people, it is easier than it sounds as it tends to be the same style of language they use when talking to you and we can just mirror this. For example, auditory people will automatically align themselves with phrases that contain words such as "sounds like", "I hear that" etc, where as a visual person will relate to sounds such as "I see that", "do you see what I mean" and "I can picture that" etc.

So what does this mean to dogs? Well, although dogs cannot understand the complexities of our language they are more than capable of having dominant emotional propensities and optimum learning tendencies. I had stated early in this book that dogs, even though scent is so important, are predominantly visual and, for most dogs, this is the case. However, not all dogs are visually prominent and some are more auditory and others by smell (olfactory). If you can understand the natural propensity of your dog then you can use this to ensure that your style of training engagement is in keeping with their natural style of learning. For example, a visual dog, such as a greyhound (or any sighthound) will decode your body language and body signals as its primary interpretation method. If this is the case, then you need to ensure that your body movements are consistent and in congruence to your instruction.

If your dog is auditory then you need to ensure that the emotion in your dialogue is in keeping with the instruction and, again, congruent. Dogs that are olfactory (smell) tend to be very treat orientated and the smellier the treat the better. Dog's that are kinaesthetic dominant will tend to be more interested in toys rather than treats.

None of the above tendencies mean that your dog will have now other tendencies as dogs can, and most do, have multiple modes but rarely will they have more than one 'dominant' modality.

Understanding your dog's learning propensities is always helpful but by no means a disaster if you feel your dog does not show any clear leaning towards one style or another. I have noted the above just to give you some reassurance that there is a lot going on in your dog and if your training efforts are not gaining the traction you were hoping for then take heart that there may be other ways available you can adopt to engage better with your dog. It is often a case of trial and error.

The first thing to do if you feel that you are struggling a bit is to take a decent break. There is nothing to be gained trying to push-on through trying different things in short succession. Taking a break and taking stock (as in the PERFECT method) can be invaluable as we, as people, often tend to skew matters with emotion when trying to analyse and assess barriers in the heat of the moment. Both you and your dog need to be in the right mental zone for effective training to take place.

Once you have had time to relax and have managed to let go of any frustration I would recommend asking yourself the following: -

1. **Is your dog too energised?** If you dog is bouncing with unexpended energy then it will not be able to focus on you no matter what the 'incentives' are. If your dog is not focused on you then you will struggle to teach or guide it effectively.

2. **Are you too energised?** If you are 'amped up' then, even though you may be motivated and focused your dog will, in all likelihood, just be focusing on your energy and may raise its own energy levels to match yours (energy transference). Dogs are fantastic at measuring and matching emotional energy to an almost to a sixth sense' level. This is a core survival skill that they have not lost and, I don't think, will ever lose.

3. **Was the environment free from distraction or distraction controlled?** Training often fails because there are too many temptations elsewhere and your dog has to show strong restraint in order to focus on you. This aspect is especially important when training your dog for a new skill as, for your dog, there will be competing priorities and, very often, temptation often wins until such times as the reward given for successfully performing the new skill become understood and embedded.

4. **Were the motivators (treats, toys etc) you chose to incentivise your dog of high enough value for your dog to focus on you to the exclusion of everything else?** Remember you are looking for a new behaviour therefore you will need to incentivise the desire for your dog to perform that new behaviour. If the reward you are offering is, in your dog's mind, not of sufficient value to motivate it to

perform (or change) then it will not perform, irrespective of what you desire.

I often get asked "are we not just bribing our dog" and my answer is both yes and no.

If you work, I assume you get paid, else why would you go to work? Well, your dog is going to work and also needs to get paid in order to keep turning up and performing. Therefore 'yes' it is a reward, a bribe, a salary or whatever you want to call it, but your dog is giving you something therefore it needs to get something back in return. The difference here is that it is always going to be performance related pay and that, for me, can never be a bad thing.

However, 'no' is equally applicable as an answer, as the aim is to (eventually) reduce or phase out the 'bribe' while still getting the desired behaviour.

The offer of a reward could be considered a training investment. For me, call it what you will but just remember that you are asking your dog to do something that, in most cases, is alien to it and unless you adequately reward your dog for doing so then it is going to be a very long and frustrating journey to get to the (behaviour) destination you want, if you get there at all.

5. **Was your dog having fun doing what you are asking for?** Everything should be a game to your dog. If your dog is not enjoying it then it is unlikely to want to do it or repeat it.

6. **Were you having fun?** This is a very important point. If training is a chore to you then it will be a chore to your dog. Neither of you will be 'up for the challenge' and the end result is likely to be failure. This is why I promote short but frequent training sessions. If you can finish a session where you and your dog want more then this will be an even greater motivator when you resume at the next session. Always leave them (and you) wanting more!

7. **Were there too many people helping you?** Too many people equals too many voices, too many opinions and too many distractions.

You are the teacher and you have your own teaching style. If there are many teachers, all with their own teaching styles, then there will be inconsistency of delivery, potential mixed messages and more than likely a confused dog. Although family and friends etc would be welcome to attend a training session, and I do recommend this, it is vital that they don't interact and leave it to you to teach one on one thus making it easier for your dog to focus directly and respond appropriately.

8. **Was your guidance clear?** Did you 'talk with purpose'? Was your vocal delivery and body language in keeping with the 5 Cs? Remember, you are teaching your dog therefore your guidance needs to be clear and unambiguous. If it is not then it will be so much harder for your dog to take on board your instruction leading to frustration and disappointment for you and your dog.

9. **Were you asking for too much too soon?** Small steps built over time equal great strides. I would recommend using the 'Kintala Principles (noted at the end of this book) when training your dog. If you try to push for too much too soon, then you may end up getting nothing at all. A small percentage improvement day on day is better than a big improvement after a short period then nothing, or inconsistent responses, thereafter.

Remember although you are teaching a behaviour you are also shaping a lifestyle. You are changing your dog's rules of engagement (primal thinking) and revising the way it lives its life. These are often major changes to a dog therefore it is always best to break matters down to the smallest elements and build things up bit by bit.

10. **Are you too tired or exasperated?** As a behaviourist, I am often called in to help when the guardians are at their "wits' end". Often a lot of what a dog specialist such as myself does is help the guardian to reset themselves provide clarity in training and reassure them that a lot of what they had invested was correct but, very often, they just needed a helping hand get over the finish line.

Good dog professionals are there to support you as much as to support your dog. There should be few 'definitive' rights or wrongs and all efforts made, even if they result in small set-backs, should be praised.

Very rarely have I attended a consultation where everything that can be done wrong has been done wrong. In a clear majority of cases, there is often a lot that has been done right. Often, the positive changes that have been achieved have not been highlighted as much as the negative behaviours which, to be honest, is very human. We, as people, tend to focus on the negative before the positive. This is unhelpful in the world of dog training.

Frustration and 'perceived' failure is tiring and it can become an ever decreasing spiral therefore, sometimes, it just needs someone to provide a bit of clarity, fresh motivation and support. When you are tired, or exasperated, it is often hard to see the wood for the trees and the seemingly obvious may elude you. This is natural and certainly not a mark of failure.

Take a break and focus on what you have achieved and not what you haven't. You will no doubt get there but to do so you must be fresh in spirit and body. Tiredness never produces good results therefore it is never a recommended state of mind to begin or continue any training.

Pacing Training

The objective of this chapter is to reassure you that set backs are normal and just part of the training and development journey. I feel it is also important to remind you that you are often asking your dog to behave in a way that is not natural for it and possibly against its own internal judgement. Dogs cannot speak our language and live within complex, confusing and fast changing environments. We, as guardians, often tower over our dogs and can be the provider of both good and bad experiences. This can be both frightening and intimidating and, I believe we have a duty of care to reassure and raise confident and happy dogs and that is why I am a supporter of positive reinforcement training.

That is also why I understand how frustrating dogs, and dog training, can be and how much it can negatively affect the family fabric. I see it first hand and I see it often. We are, mostly, all trying to do what we feel is right for our dog but oftentimes we just don't know what right is. There can be no judgement or criticism in this. It is alright to fall over. It is alright to ask for help. It is alright to love your dog as much as you do your family. No matter what, if you have the welfare of your dog at heart and don't use force or fear then it is all alright.

Another key point is that you should not let 'dog training' consume your life. It is vitally important that dog training works around your lifestyle and not the other way around. It is so easy to 'fall-out-of-love' with dog training which can quickly escalate to falling-out-of-love with your dog. It needn't be, nor should it be, like this. Just like you have a work-life balance you should also have a dog-life balance. If you have kids you no doubt have some 'me time' (if not, you really should) to retain your sanity and stop you from saying or doing something out of frustration and the same should be true of the relationship you have with your dog. It is all about balance. If you have a plan or objective then that should be enough. It is a marathon not a sprint and the 'breaks' between training, and thinking about training, are as equally important as the training itself. Dog training is a life choice and real results are built up from getting small wins. Remember, to motivate your dog you first need to motivate yourself so plan your dog-life balance accordingly.

In the next, and final, chapter (Seeking Professional Support) I will detail the recommended approach should you feel that you require a dog professional to give you some additional support.

'MANAGING SET BACKS' CHAPTER SUMMARY

- **Frustration**
- **Ticking all the right boxes**
- **NLP and dogs**
- **Take a break**
- **Reflection on training**
- **Unnatural behaviour**
- **Pacing training**
- **Seeking further support**

Chapter 8: Seeking Professional Support

It must be said that even after reading this book, and possibly many other books, that you may still wish to seek help and support to change some particularly undesired behaviour in your dog. This should not be seen as a point of defeat as, with the best will in the world, some dogs just don't respond to our efforts no matter what we try.

This is where you may consider getting a dog professional involved. A good dog professional will be able to apply a more personal bespoke solution taking into consideration the unique character and temperament of your dog as well as the environment which it lives within. There will, no doubt, be lots of good dog professionals around you and will only ever be an internet search away.

A quick word of warning though, I have met many fellow dog professionals who are absolutely passionate about all things dog but seemingly not-so-much when it comes to all things people, but, for me, I would want someone who is both.

The above being the case who do you call? Disappointingly, dog training and behaviour modification is currently unregulated and anybody can call themselves a professional dog trainer. This makes engaging a competent professional a bit of a minefield.

To add to the confusion there are currently two <u>established</u> methodologies in respect of how to teach dogs or modify their behaviour. The 'old school' principles of being the 'alpha' and using 'dominance' methods which, even today, is still practised and prevalent. This style of training has no doubt been helped in part from the likes of Cesar Millan and his 'the Dog Whisperer' TV programs.

The other is, as detailed in this book, positive reinforcement training (P+) as promoted by me and the likes of leading eminent practitioners such as Dr Ian Dunbar, Zak George, Steve Mann and Victoria Stilwell to name but a few. I very much align myself within this positive reinforcement camp.

That being said, I am not one of those who wish to vilify the likes of Cesar Millan as I think to do so totally misses the point. I believe that Cesar Millan, who has decades of dog behaviour experience, does have the welfare of dogs at the heart of everything he does. Cesar Millan has been the rescuer for many dogs and families where he has helped them positively transform their lives resulting in keeping the families together and thus saving the lives of many dogs. Let me be clear Cesar Milan has saved the lives of countless dogs and helped many families with their doggy challenges.

I just don't agree with his 'style' and the 'mechanics' of applying 'alpha' and 'dominance' techniques as I feel that not only do they rely on force and fear to get results but they could easily be misunderstood/misinterpreted and become a gateway for increased physical and psychological abuse against dogs. It is for this reason that there is a disclaimer at the start of every Dog Whisperer program. For me, anything that requires a disclaimer should always be treated with caution. Dog training is for everybody and should always be engaging, fun and safe. The exception to the rule is when working with dogs that are aggressive, or have a history of aggression or attacks, where more specialist support will be required. Looking for professional support may be required for non-aggressive dogs too. You may have a dog that is just not responding to any training program you have tried therefore you just need a dog professional to give you, via their knowledge and experience, some hints and tips on what you can do to achieve better results. That is perfectly reasonable and the responsible thing to do.

I am an advocate for force free training and development as, for me, it makes more sense and is in keeping with my personal principles. I would rather have a dog wanting to work with me instead of it being fearful of me. My dogs, Darcy and Piper, and even the ones I work with, I view as part of my extended family (pack) and I like to think that I have an emotional bond with each and every one of them. I need them, and their guardians, to have trust in me in order for me to help them learn new things and/or change past behaviours. I work hard to promote and maintain this harmonious relationship ethos at every opportunity.

With the above principles in mind, I have put together some tips which should allow you to effectively vet potential dog professionals before you shortlist, book and/or engage with them. My 10 tips noted below should reduce the risk of getting an unsuitable practitioner considerably.

1. **Force Free / Science based**: The potential dog professional should encompass the principles of changing behaviour via rewarding good behaviour (using treats, toys and praise as reinforcers) with no pain, no force, no fear involved.

   If, during the initial dialogue, they refer to using *alpha* or *dominance* techniques or mention being the 'pack leader' then they are likely to be "old-school" in philosophy and use the tools of 'force and fear' rather than incentivising and motivating behaviour changes as this book recommends. Furthermore, they are likely to use control tools, such as choke chains, e-collars, sprays etc, which may treat the symptoms but never the cause, and which I would never advocate.

   Dogs have been studied more now than they ever had been previously and from these studies a lot of myths have been debunked and a lot of new ways of working with your dog have been developed.

Positive reinforcement trainers tend to use modern, science-based methods and tend to have a greater understanding of dog motivation techniques.

Dr Ian Dunbar was an early pioneer of this new way of thinking and developed such programs as 'Sirius'® puppy training which, I believe, was the forerunner of the positive reinforcement movement. From this, modern practitioners such as Zak George, Steve Mann, Tom Mitchell, Lauren Langman and many others have built their reputations on the back of these principles, as have I. In fact, Zak George has coined this as a 'Dog Training Revolution'® and who am I to disagree?

2. **Qualifications & Experience**: Make sure that they have some current and relevant qualifications. Check with the issuing bodies to ensure that these are valid. Also enquire what continuous learning they have completed recently (continued Professional Development (CPD))? Most bona fide professionals will be committed to lifelong learning and it is often a requirement of their original qualification certification authority. If you can, find out as much as you can from websites such as 'dogtime', or 'dogs101' about the breed history, characteristics and

temperament of your dog and test the professionals understanding of your dog's breed.

The dog professional should have some general breed knowledge and should also be prepared to do some research on your dog's specific breed before they attend. It is important that the dog professional does some research as new information is generated daily about all things dog, including breed information, and you will want them to have 'current' up-to-date understanding and knowledge. In addition, many breeds are cross and not pure therefore they will need to have a good understanding of the potential mix types in your dog.

3. **Reviews**: Don't get fooled by someone who has a lot of reviews, even if they are all 5* reviews as fake online reviews is, unfortunately, an increasing problem nowadays.

    Read the content of the reviews to see if these are detailed, look genuine or have clues about the style of their approach. Further, look for reviews from more than one site and look for 'cut and paste' content from same, or similarly, written reviews from one site to another. True reviews tend to be site specific and reviews on other sites that seemed to be copied may just be that, so be aware. Lastly, look at the dates of when the reviews were made. If a lot of reviews were completed within a short period of time and then nothing, or next to nothing, has been written thereafter then this should raise a flag.

4. **Personality**: Do you feel that the practitioner has built a rapport with you? Have they focused on themselves rather than you and your challenges? Do you feel that they are listening to you? If you don't bond with them initially do not expect this to change much if you engage them. Remember, if they cannot sell themselves to you (without you having reservations) then how will they sell their solutions to you after you have engaged them?

5. **Provide instant diagnosis**: This is one of my pet hates. Does the dog professional provide definitive and instant diagnosis over-the-phone or by email without having taken the time to understand you, your dog and, equally as important, the environment? If so, they are providing a diagnosis without substance and it is likely they are not aware of the full facts and circumstances.

A good professional should always refrain from definitive statements and diagnosis until such times as they have had a chance to conclude an in-situ consultation. Think about it, you would not expect your doctor to diagnose you without seeing you therefore, I believe, it should be no different for dog professionals. General hypotheses yes, but definitive solutions and prognosis, not-so-much.

6. **Can they offer a range of solutions**: Taking the principle of general hypothesis a step further can they assure you that there is not only one way to deal with the issue, or issues?

What you do not want to do is engage with someone who provides a one-size-fits-all program that is masquerading as bespoke or, even worse, they provide a diagnosis that relies on assumption and not fact.

In addition, are they making claims or statements that seem overly simplistic, overly complicated or too good to be true? If so, tread with caution. A good professional should work hard to understand you and your situation and ask more questions than you. If that is not the case then how can they fully understand your situation?

7. **Do they understand YOUR situation**? As alluded to in point 6 how can a dog professional fully understand your situation if they do not probe you more than you probe them?

They may know about dogs but you know about your dog and your circumstances and that, for me, takes precedence in painting a full picture.

As a dog professional I have years of experience and knowledge which I can call upon but what I don't know is what I will be walking into. I want to flesh out as much as I can before I start referencing and applying my knowledge and solutions. I do this via my pre-visit questionnaire but other practitioners may have their own way of obtaining key information before they attend. If they don't require pre-visit information from you then they are, effectively, walking in blind, and that can often be a recipe for, continued but unnecessary visits, or even actual disaster.

Another important point, for me, as it is another pet hate, is are they talking down to you or conducting a conversation riddled with jargon? Often jargon is used as a 'I know better than you' barrier with the objective of stopping you asking questions. This places you on the backfoot thinking that your questions are, or will be, daft questions. They are not and, irrespective of whether or not you think your question is a daft question basically, if you think it ask it!

8. **Do they offer follow on support**: I am not a fan of the 'attend once and move on' school of trainer support. As stated, once I get involved I have a bond and commitment with the dog and its family and I like to become part of the journey.

   Things don't always pan out the way they were planned but that is the benefit of maintaining the support because you can review progress and revise if required. Therefore, I like to always plan, at the very least, one follow-up visit and witness, first hand, the progress of the agreed program.

   I would also expect to give my clients a written summary or report of my consultation as I will impart a lot of information at the consultation and I would not expect my client to stand their taking notes or committing everything to memory.

9. **Bang for your buck**: It is hard to place a true value on the work a good dog professional does because I

believe the difference a good one can make is priceless. However, money is not limitless and you need to ensure that you get what you pay for. In this respect, find out what is included in their fee. Does it include just a home visit, a written report, a follow up visit or any equipment you may need. Make sure all costs are stated up front so there are no surprises.

A warning though, don't just go on price. Ask yourself, are they too expensive or too cheap? You are purchasing the time and knowledge of someone who has spent years learning their trade therefore this will come at a cost. If a price seems too good to be true then it probably is and this may be a teaser price with add-ons to follow.

Try not to get caught in a price entrapment scenario. Get at least 3 quotes and study what is included in each quote.

10. ***TRUST YOUR INSTINCTS!*** Pragmatism is one thing but intuition is another. Your gut instinct is rarely wrong and it has come to a conclusion (gut feeling) by subliminally processing a lot of information that you may not even be aware of. Intuition is, as it is in many animals including dogs, your survival instinct and is primed to protect you

therefore if your gut says something is not quite right, even if you don't know what it is, then trust it and move on.

The above tips and the content of this book will enable you to engage any dog professional from a position of knowledge thus allowing you to converse confidently with them. In addition, after you have engaged someone make sure that before they leave that you are happy and confident in what you have to do. If not, ask for clarification or more information as once the professional leaves then you are on your own.

'SEEKING PROFESSIONAL SUPPORT' CHAPTER SUMMARY

- **Unregulated sector**
- **Leading practitioners**
- **10 tips on engaging a dog professional**
- **Confidence in engaging a dog professional**

The Kintala Principles

Pawsitive Changes the Kintala Way

1. We lead our dog by learning its language
2. We guide calmly in all situations
3. We incentivise change we don't demand it
4. We work at our dog's pace not ours

We become one with our dog

Patience, understanding, dedication and small steps equal great strides!

How to contact or find out more about me: -

Email: info@dencooke.com

Website: https://dencooke.com/

Instagram https://www.instagram.com/dencooke

You Tube: https://www.youtube.com/ (search Den Cooke)

Facebook: https://www.facebook.com/pawsitiveden

References

Over and above my knowledge, experience and continued professional development I have noted below just some of the other sources I have drawn from in writing this book. The list is an indicative extract and is in no particular order. In addition, I am not stating that I particularly agree, or disagree, with the theories or philosophies of the authors listed.

Book /Course Title	Author
Inside of a Dog: What Dogs See, Smell, and Know	Alexandra Horowitz
Dog Training Revolution	Zak George
Guide to a Well Behaved Dog	Zak George
Simple Solutions for Common Dog Behaviour and Training Problems	Dr Ian Dunbar
Before and After Getting Your Puppy	Dr Ian Dunbar
If Your Dog Could Talk	Dr Bruce Fogle
In Defence of Dogs	John Bradshaw
Brain Games for Dogs	Claire Arrowsmith
The Perfect Dog	Dr Roger Mugford
IMDT / IMDTB	Steve Mann
Easy Peasy Puppy Squeezy	Steve Mann
Easy Peasy Doggy Squeezy	Steve Mann
How to Train a Superdog	Gwen Bailey
How to Speak Dog	Stanley Coren
The Dog's Mind: Understanding Your Dog's Brain	

	Dr Bruce Fogle
Why Does my Dog Do That?	Caroline Spencer
Inside Your Dog's Mind	Victoria Stilwell
Behaviour Adjustment Training 2.0	Grisha Stewart
Clever Dog: Understand What Your Dog is Telling You	
	Sarah Whitehead
Cesar Millan's Guide to a Happy Dog	Cesar Millan
Cesar's Way	Cesar Millan
Chemical Communication in Domestic Dogs	
	Dr Anneke Lisberg
	(Lisberg & Snowden (2009)

Printed in Great Britain
by Amazon

52812285R00169